I0487677

The GopherHaul Lawn Care Marketing & Landscaping Business Show Episode Guide.

By Steve Low

Host of the GopherHaul Show.

Contents

The Adventurers.

Foreward

A little history.

Hello everyone and welcome to GopherHaul! If you haven't started your business yet, what are you waiting for. If you don't start your business this year, you'll be at least one year older when you do, so get started today!

The GopherHaul show and book have been an absolutely blast so far to create. A bunch of years back, we started up a forum for Gopher Lawn Care Business Software support. With all the lawn care business owners it attracted, it then morphed into a lawn care business forum.

Sometime in the summer of 2006, Anthony who is one of our forum members, shared with us that he was experimenting with creating horror films and putting small updates on youtube. That got me thinking why not create a show about the forum that helps lawn care business owners and thus GopherHaul, the show, was created.

Since then, I have put out twenty six GopherHaul episodes, with over 1,000,000 views and I really think they are getting better as I go. I am constantly learning new business tips and tricks through the Gopher forum. I love sharing all that I have learned with everyone and I hope this episode guide puts all of the content discussed over the course of the first 26 episodes into an easily digestible format.

If you have business questions, get on the Gopher Forum, introduce yourself and say hi. If you need free lawn care business contracts, proposals, flyers, door hangers, website templates, logos, customer letters, they are all on the site too. Also don't forget to listen to our GopherHaul lawn care business podcasts.

Check out our lawn care business blog at http://www.lawnchat.com.

If we inspire you to get your own business started, please share your story with us. Your story will then become an inspiration for future entrepreneurs!

Thanks for watching GopherHaul, or reading in this case and always remember to Dream it, Build it, Gopher it!

Sincerely, Steve Low

Continue your reading.

I have more great information on running a lawn care business in my other book, "**Stop Lowballing! A Lawn Care Business Owner's Guide To Success.**"

Some of the topics discussed in the book: - How to start up your lawn care business. - Finding your niche and finding profits. - Lawn Care Equipment. - Pricing & Estimating Lawn Care Jobs. - Dealing With Customers. - Dealing With Employees. - Lawn Care Marketing Secrets. - Lawn Care Business Tips. - Getting Commercial Accounts without commercial references. - Pitfalls of Commercial Accounts. And more.

You can order this book through our website http://www.gophersoftware.com or on amazon.com.

Special thanks to Gopher Lawn Care Software.

This book would not have been possible without the help and guidance of all our friends and business owners we have met over the years on our forum as well as others. As with everything, this book is a work in progress. If you would like to contribute some of your thoughts and reflections on it, please send them to us via our forum or email support@gophersoftware.com.

Also thank you to the staff at Gopher Software for making all of this possible.

Lawn Care Software
PROBLEM: Scheduling & billing repetitive jobs is tedious and time consuming.
SOLUTION: Gopher Billing & Scheduling Software allows you to Quickly and Easily schedule jobs and create invoices.

Gopher Landscape Billing and Scheduling Software simplifies the task of scheduling your lawn care jobs and billing your customers. Simply set up your jobs at the beginning of the season and let Gopher handle the rest. With Gopher, you can print out a list of scheduled jobs for each day and then automatically print invoices after those jobs have been completed.

Download your free trial of Gopher Billing & Scheduling Software at
http://www.gophersoftware.com

GopherHaul 2

Overview of GopherHaul

Episode 2

Original Air Date: Sept. 21, 2006

In this episode we discussed.
* Getting started marketing your new lawn care business.

Getting started marketing your new lawn care business.

In this episode we talk about marketing basics for the lawn care operator. When you are first getting started in business something you should think about is how are you going to position your company, through marketing.

When we talk about marketing, we are talking about anything you do to get attention for your company and hopefully attract business because of your efforts. Another thing you should consider is will you be marketing your company on **price**, on **quality** or **personalized service**?

Personalize Service

* Marketing on personalized service means you are going to position your company as one who provides higher end custom services and you will be charging more for these services. You the owner will be the one answering phone calls when the customer has a problem. You will personally service the customers yard and take care of all their lawn care needs. Your potential customers will be looking for personalized service and be willing to pay a premium for it.

Quality

* Marketing on quality service means you will be promoting your

company as artisans. Your company can perform services that newer companies just don't have the skill to do.

Price

- Marketing on price means you are going to promote how low your prices are compared to other businesses in the area. You will be looking for the customer who cares first and foremost about price over service or quality.

When you are developing your marketing platform, consider these different concepts. Use the one that best describes your company. You can also mix and match them as needed.

When you are first starting off in the business world, you need cash flow and most likely you haven't developed the skill set to know what a high end customer will want or how to provide such services, so that is why many lawn care operators work from the ground floor and build up.

Most lawn care operators start out marketing on price. Your costs as a start up will most likely be lower than if you are an established company. Because your costs will be lower, you can charge a lower price and still make a profit.

As you grow you will learn more skills and techniques to become specialized and be able to charge a premium for those services.

A few words of warning: When you market on price, remember there will always be another company willing to beat your price and put themselves out of business faster than you. Marketing on price is a quick start way to get business but you need to move out of that as soon as you can. Many times new lawn care operators say they want to become the Wal-mart of the lawn care industry. If you are thinking about this, ask yourself, how are you going to be able to compete on price with a 12 year old who charges $5 to mow a neighbors lawn while using the neighbor's lawn mower. **You can't always be the lowest price.**

If you use this as your marketing strategy to get yourself started, you will need to learn about the industry asap so you can develop specialized skills which will allow you to charge a premium for your time in the future.

Let's look at marketing on price.

Here is a sample template from our free collection of download templates.

We can see this template says give us a try, 1st lawn cut $25.00. Your goal when using such a door hanger is that the potential customer is looking for cheap service they can jump on and see how you do. Make sure you put an expiration date on the offer or you might be surprised when you get calls on this deal a year from now when you are no longer interested in offering the service at this price.

Another coupon on this door hanger offers a free lawn cut with any spring cleanup. You could use such a coupon in the spring or change it to be used in the fall as well. The goal of this coupon is to catch the customer when they might be doing their own mowing throughout the year but do not want to put the work into cleaning their yard in the spring and fall. If you impress them with your abilities, you might get them to sign on as a weekly customer in the future.

The middle coupon offers 2 free lawn cuts with a maintenance agreement. Your maintenance agreement will most likely be for a 1 year duration. If you need one of them, you can download a lawn care contract template for free from our website http://www.getgopher.com.

Some lawn care operators like to use contracts others don't. If you choose to use one, remember, if the customer becomes unhappy with your service, they will stop using your company and then it will be up to you to enforce the contract which may not be something you want to do. Taking a customer to court always has the potential for causing bad word of mouth for you and your company.

Remember to include your contact information and list all the services you provide in your marketing material.

Another flyer to use when you are marketing on price is this one.

This one is very basic and asks the question are you paying too much for lawn maintenance?

It goes on to show the cost of cutting the lawn per week. When you use such flyers, make sure you know your hourly operating expenses otherwise you might find yourself losing money and not even knowing it until it's too late.

Also make sure you know how long it will take to service the lawns you are quoting at $25.00. Don't put yourself in a situation where you are cutting large lawns at a loss and only do a few smaller lawns at a profit. Consider leaving the price area blank when you print out the flyer and then later write the price in with a pen when you are on site so you can evaluate the lawn to determine how much you should charge.

Here is a door hanger design we created for one or our friends on the Gopher Lawn Care Business Forum. In this design we show him on the door hanger.
We are promoting him and his personalized service.
We want the potential customer to see who will be cutting their lawn even before they make the first call to contact him. In this picture, Joe is striking a friendly and confident pose. He is letting the potential customer know he has the skill and ability to get the job done right. You can also see the white circle which allows Joe to write down a price on the door hanger as he hands them out. Each price is based on the yard he surveys as he walks up to the front door. When the potential customer sees this door hanger they will not only know who owns the company, which is reassuring, but they will know what the price will be for the service.

If you are interested in using this door hanger, the design is available for free download on our site http://www.getgopher.com

In the template we did take Joe's picture out so you can put your own one in.

When you want to position your company as high quality and higher priced, you probably are a more established and have been in business for a while. You have a better idea of what you are doing and have the technical know how to do jobs newer companies may not be able to easily perform.

You might decide to use a door hanger like this one.

It promotes a high quality professional looking service company. Notice the person in the image is wearing a company uniform and looks professional. The yard looks nice and the grass lush. You will also notice there is no price on the door hanger. When you are marketing a high quality service, you really want the potential customer to call you so you can set up an appointment to review their property and talk with the client to explain what they are getting when they hire you. Only at the end of the sales pitch would you tell them the price.

I hope this marketing discussion has helped you grow. Keep in mind, your marketing campaign is not going to be a one hit wonder. Don't do it once and expect to find customers pounding on your door. There is a lot of competition and you need to keep getting your name out there.

GopherHaul 4

Overview of GopherHaul

Episode 4

Original Air Date: Nov. 18, 2006

In this episode we discussed.
- The 6 deadly lawn care marketing mistakes.

The 6 deadly lawn care marketing mistakes.

I had a great discussion with Chestin of lawncaremarketingmagic.com and he shared with us his list of the 6 deadly marketing mistakes. I added some of my insights to this list as well.

1. Don't copy big business.

2. Don't confuse branding with marketing.
   - When you are getting started, you shouldn't be focused on getting people to know your brand name as much as you should be focusing on getting customers by servicing their needs. Don't put your logo at the top of your flyers. Instead put the problems your lawn care business will solve at the top of the flyer. For example, give them *more free time to spend with their family on weekends*.

3. Don't ask your marketing material to do too much.
   - Basically this means don't expect one piece of marketing material to move a customer from step A to step Z. There is a process you must take to transition a potential customer to becoming a customer.

4. Not asking enough from your marketing material.
   - Your marketing should move your potential customer from step A to step B.

5. Not selecting a niche.
   - Chestin explains you can't be all things to all people. So ask

yourself, what services can you do that stand out from your competitors and promote them.

6. Not standing out.
   - How are you differentiating yourself from your competition? Chestin feels this is the biggest mistake of them all. If you are unable to differentiate yourself from other competitors you will end up in price wars with them. This is not something you want to do if you plan on building a successful long term business.

Chestin feels that direct marketing is the key to success. No other form of marketing is as trackable, scalable or cost effective as direct marketing.

If you do decide to use direct marketing for your lawn care business, remember to track the responses. How? Put tracking codes in your offers. Make sure the customer gives you the code when calling to get that special price or have them present you the coupon with the tracking code on it. Then you will know which offers are working or which ones aren't. When you find one that works, you can then scale up your marketing by sending out more marketing materials to others homes in your service area.

GopherHaul 5

Overview of GopherHaul
Episode 5

Original Air Date: Dec. 16, 2006

In this episode we discussed.
- The best way to collect contact information through your website?

The best way to collect contact information through your website?

In this episode we talked about our collection of free lawn care business web templates that are available for download. Once you get your website up and running, you will then want to collect contact information from people who visit your site. This helps you build up a list of potential customers who you can send further marketing material to with the goal of turning them into customers.

The first thing you need to do when you want to collect contact information is to offer the reader something valuable in return. What can you offer in return? How about free reports emailed to them. Or free newsletters full of information they would be interested in reading. Your report could be entitled "5 secrets to achieving a beautiful, lush, green lawn." This might get a homeowner interested in giving you their contact information. In your report you would tell them what to do to achieve such a lush lawn without telling them how to do it. This is ultimately where you would step in as the expert.

On your website you can set up an auto-responder. This would allow the potential customer to fill in their contact information and have it submitted to your database, then it would automatically send them an emailed response. This response would be your first report. Then you could send them monthly new reports or newsletters that would educate them further on lawn care. Also you could send out mass emailings of specials you are offering throughout the year. Early season specials like '_sign up now and prepay your lawn care for the entire year and save 10%. Act fast, this offer is only available until xx/xx/xx._' Can you imagine what the response rate would be when you have a list of customers who all need lawn care service and are already familiar with you and your website?

GopherHaul 6

Overview of GopherHaul

Episode 6

Original Air Date: Jan. 18, 2007

In this episode we discussed.
* What's better to use, postcards or brochures?

What's better to use, postcards or brochures?

Here is a great question that came into the forum and I am thankful our friend Chestin from lawncaremarketingmagic.com was able to jump in here and give us such a great response.

Question: "What do you feel is a better marketing tool, postcards or brochures? I feel with brochures I can get more information to the potential customers, such as all the services I provide as well as some photos of some of my customer's lawns. What do think?"

Answer: "As you no doubt know, sending brochures is much more expensive than postcards, but as you stated, they allow you to tell a much more complete story and include more of things like photos, testimonials, etc. If your budget allows, I would certainly suggest going the brochure route.

If you do decide to go that way, keep these tips in mind when creating your brochure:

* If possible, definitely include some pictures of your work but don't crowd it with too many pictures. Leave some room for your sales message.
* Don't be afraid to use lots of text to tell your story and deliver your sales message. If you were sending a salesman to their door, you wouldn't limit him to 250 words or less, would you? Definitely not and you don't want to do the same to your marketing collateral.

- Be sure to start your brochure off with an attention grabbing headline. Just because they receive it doesn't mean they're going to read it. You need to give them some reasons for reading.
- Don't just list your services or features. Everything you say MUST be as much about the potential customer as possible, so take everything you think you want to say about all the services you offer and translate those into benefits for the customer. (Example: 15 years experience – We have the knowledge and experience necessary to ensure the job gets done right the FIRST time and without any unnecessary problems or expense)
- Present an offer that invites them to contact you for additional information or for a low-risk trial of your services. If you're going to spend any money on producing these brochures, you'd be silly NOT to make them some type of offer that gets them to at least contact you for more information.
- If you have some customer testimonials, use them. Just as with the pictures, letting your satisfied customers tell the story will go a long way towards reducing the skepticism felt by your prospects.
- Give them a number of different ways to respond and then tell them exactly how you'd like them to respond. For example, give them your office number and tell them to call during the hours of 8am – 5pm. Or give them your website and tell them to log on and fill out the 'Request an Estimate' form. Don't assume they know what they need to do to respond. You need to tell them specifically."

GopherHaul 7

Overview of GopherHaul

Episode 7

Original Air Date: Feb. 11, 2007

In this episode we discussed.
- Building your customer base with referrals.

Building your customer base through referrals.

Many successful lawn care businesses find their greatest resource to get new customers is through their current customer base. In a forum discussion we talked about the best ways to attract referrals through your current customer base.

Steve: "What is your view on the offer of free mowing, is it something you think lawn care business owners should be offering this spring?"

Bob: "I don't like to get involved in that issue too much. Too many people have very strong beliefs on not giving free apps/cuts, no discounts because of "lowballing" but if it gets a customer I say do it. You have to look at the life of the customer. If it costs you $50 one year and you retain them for 5, then what's the harm. More so than anything your marketing material needs to to get the customer to pick up the phone!!"

Steve: "Do you have other suggestions of offers that can help other lawn care business owners gain new customers?"

Bob: "Here is an idea for getting customers. Use a tear-off postage paid business reply postcard. In it, ask your customers to give you a referral. When the referral signs up your customer gets money! The difference is, instead of a simply credited their lawn care account (credit is still offered), give them the option. I give "$25.00 Visa Gift Cards." Give them a "good" reason to refer a friend. FREE MONEY is better than a credit on their account. A credit is nice, but a

Gift Card in the mailbox from their lawn care company makes more of an impact. My second choice was a Home Depot gift card, every homeowner goes to home depot. I'll bet there isn't a lawn care business owner in the world that wouldn't pay $25 for every single new account."

This is a very interesting idea! When you think about how much it costs to acquire a new customer, you might find $25 is actually a very cheap way to do it.

GopherHaul 8

Overview of GopherHaul

Episode 8

Original Air Date: April 4, 2007

In this episode we discussed.
- How to make a killer spring lawn care flyer.

How to make a killer spring lawn care flyer.

Spring is here and lawn care companies from around the world are looking for ways to make a killer flyer to attract new customers. How are you gonna do this? Well don't worry, we got you covered.

Flyers are great method of advertising because they are cheap, easy to make, and easy to distribute. The first thing you want on your flyer is a catchy headline. Remember if you don't catch the readers eyes immediately, they are most likely going to throw the flyer away without even reading it. In this flyer we ask the reader if they would like a thick, lush and healthy lawn. Then we tell them with our help it will be easy.

- Next in smaller print we give the reader our sales pitch.
- We have a limited time offer of a free soil test for the first x amount of callers who call before a specific date. This is designed to get the reader to act now.
- We include a list of other services we offer.
- At the bottom we have our logo and contact information along with a

couple of coupons.
- Also point out you offer free estimates and that you are fully insured.

One of the biggest mistakes we see in flyer designs is that a lawn care business owner will put their logo and company name at the top with huge letters. Now before you do that, ask yourself, how is that going to help catch the readers eye? I know you are proud of your company and your company logo. I am proud of you too, but remember we are trying to catch new customers and the bait we need to do that is a headline that has a good hook. Logos go at the bottom and headlines go at the top. If you want to use this flyer or any of our other flyer or doorhanger designs, **you can download them for free** by going to http://www.getgopher.com

GopherHaul 9

Overview of GopherHaul

Episode 9

Original Air Date: May 4, 2007

In this episode we discussed.
- Overhaul of a new start up lawn care business.

New business owner needs an overhaul.

Lee has got to be one of my favorite lawn care business owners I have met on the Gopher Lawn Care Business Forum. I talk about him and his business in much more detail later in this book. I think his story is just so fantastic because it was a great example of the meteoric rise you can find if you aren't afraid to experiment with marketing concepts. I hope by sharing this story with you, it will inspire you to go out there explore and experiment yourself.

Lee: "I am new to the lawn care and property management business. I am retired military and worked for FedEx for 14 years. I guess I just got tired of working for someone else for all those years. I am going to attempt to establish a good reputation for quality work.

I am finding it difficult to break in. I have been reading and studying the market. I have done all the right things with a small budget. If anyone has any suggestions as to how to make my business grow faster please drop me a line. Heck if you are in my area and have too much work or need a hand let me know. To all of you that post on this forum thanks for all the great information. I enjoy the read."

Steve: "Welcome to our forum!

I think a biggie is to leverage something that makes you unique and use it to stand out.

What kinds of things have you been doing as far as marketing thus far?

What kinds of future ideas were you planning on doing to get the word out?"

Lee: "I have been using flyers on mail boxes so far but I am getting only a few phone calls. It feels like some days I can put out 100 flyers and get 3 or 4 calls and then I put out a 1000 and get none.

I have plans on getting signs for my truck and a website.

Just starting out I have a small budget so any help and suggestions would be helpful and welcomed."

Steve: "Lee, first off, keep in mind, if you put flyers in or on a mailbox, you may get a call from the local post master. As far as **response rates from flyers**, most of the time it seems a **1 or 2% response is on average** what you will get.

I think since you are starting with a small budget, you should leverage your time to get attention. Since you were in the military, here are some ideas.

What if you got involved with the program that helps maintain lawns in your area of military members over seas? Is that possible? You could then put together a press release on how you are retired military and tell your story and then show how you are helping military members now.

Maybe the paper could help find military households in need of your assistance? This could be a great way to build up word of mouth and goodwill in your community.

Also have you been handing out business cards to everyone you know?"

Lee: "That is a great idea about assisting military members. As you might know that some could really use the help. I think I will go out to the local base and see if they will do a release. I also have friends at the local paper that could help get the word out.

The over all plan is to break even this year. Then, next year have it take off. I am hoping to have about a $10,000 budget at the beginning of next season."

Steve: "Growing your business is a lot like growing a garden. It is very difficult to force growth.

The more you get involved with your community, the more your name will be out there. This will help you land more accounts.

I think with you especially it's great to work with the military because of your connection. Have you attempted to create any flyers or door hangers which will promote that part of you as well? Could we see some of your promotional material?

I really like your name Tiger Time Lawn Care. You could also build up the brand by playing with the name in your marketing material. What if you added a tiger fur colored theme to your trucks? Maybe make it safari like? This would be helpful to stand out from the pack. Maybe your uniform could even be like that of zoo workers?

Keep thinking how to create a theme and a brand. How to stand out!"

Lee: "I had thought about the tiger theme on my truck and lawn equipment. I had not thought about the attire idea. I have to keep some of the thought down because of the budget right now. I seem to be growing at a steady pace but it still seems slow to me. I have 16 accounts right now but I was hoping for 30 by now. I am thinking that before summer is over I will have at least 50.

As soon as my budget will allow me, I am going to paint the truck. I thought about getting signs with the theme as well, however playing with it on my computer it was hard to read.

I am working on a small movie to add to the website that plays Eye of the Tiger while showing information about the lawn care service.

What would Zoo apparel cost? I am about to start hiring some people to help in the business."

Steve: "Now here is an idea of what you could do to get attention. I bet it could be done for fairly cheap. Get a $100 truck painting in orange and then you could use tape to stencil in the stripes. Paint them with spray paint if you wanted in black.

Then put your vinyl lettering on the side and WOW would this stand out! "

Lee: "That would draw a ton of attention and laughter, however the truck would be remembered and that is for sure. I think it would be a idea that would draw business."

Steve: "We all have to be self-promoters. Some of us will take self-promotion to new levels and really stand out. Those who do will benefit from that attention.

Many other business owners will not want to go too 'crazy.' But then we risk falling into the pool of sameness as we do not differentiate ourselves from others."

Lee: "See, I think your right. You have to stand out from the crowd or you are the same as everyone else. You can give a quality product all day long but if you are "Joe bag of dough nuts lawn care service" well that is what you will be looked upon as.

I am happy to hear that you like the name. I am getting positive responses to it. I got my first two commercial contracts yesterday. Do ya want to know why? The name Tiger Time. LOL funny how things work."

Steve: "Here is a marketing idea for Tiger Time. Maybe others could use this as well.

What you could do is, paint your truck with the tiger stripes then create some flyers with the truck's picture on it. Put these flyers around your town. At the top of the flyer you could say 'Have you seen this truck?' Offer a reward if someone has seen your truck and they either call you or email you.

Then come up with a reward like maybe a free lawn mowing with an annual maintenance agreement or maybe a free lawn care analysis which includes soil testing.

You could call the person back with this reward offer or email them.

What are your thoughts on this? Do you think it would create a buzz? What if you took out a newspaper ad that did the same thing too? I bet if you drove around town after the ad was placed you would get a ton of calls.

You could then work on converting those callers to becoming customers."

Troy: "The only problem, they might think that it's stolen."

Steve: "Very true. It's edgy."

Troy: "It's a very good idea. It could either be very good or be a nightmare. That will definitely grab the attention of customers. I would love hear the success of doing that to his truck."

You can join in on the discussions here

http://www.gophergraphics.com/forum/cgi-bin/ikonboard.cgi?act=ST;f=26;t=4825

and here

http://www.gophergraphics.com/forum/cgi-bin/ikonboard.cgi?act=ST;f=8;t=4851

As you continue in your reading, you will see how Lee harnessed his creativity and took his lawn care business to unheard of levels of media attention. If you could only harness a tiny percentage of what Lee was able to do with the media, you would be a smashing success.

GopherHaul 10

Overview of GopherHaul

Episode 10

Original Air Date: June 5, 2007

In this episode we discussed.
- Gain one customer then lose one customer. What can I do to stop it?
- How to pre-screen customers when they call?
- Using high fuel prices to attract new customers.

I gain one customer then lose one customer. How can I stop it?

Gman started off this discussion on the Gopher Lawn Care Forum by asking this question. I am always getting new customers, but then I lose 1. There seems to be a big turnover all the time. Is this how it is in the lawn biz? Just wondering if this is normal or am i doing something wrong?

Steve: "Are these weekly service customers you are talking about or are you referring to one time jobs like clean ups etc?"

Gman: "These are not cleanups, they are weekly customers."

Chestin from lawncaremarketingmagic.com: "It could be your customers are leaving because they're having a hard time equating the cost you're charging with the value they're receiving. As a result, when someone else comes along with a cheaper price (and lesser service), they drop you like an old boyfriend.

The key is to make sure they understand the VALUE they're receiving as a result of your service. It could be the extra attention you pay their yard, or the years of experience you have in the industry, or the fact that you're licensed and insured. Each of these facts translates into some benefit for your customer and it's your job to make sure they understand what that benefit is.

Also, even though this may cause some debate among LCO's, I firmly believe it's vital that you establish a relationship with your customers. Get to know them beyond the services you provide and take an interest in their lives. That doesn't mean invite yourself over for dinner, but consider sending a monthly newsletter, birthday or holiday cards, calling periodically to check on things, etc.

Go that extra step to make them feel important and the next time a cheaper offer comes along, they'll think long and hard about dropping you."

Steve: "Chestin, If a lawn care business owner goes about asking customers who are leaving why they are leaving, should they ask if it is because of a lack of value?

How would you suggest an owner ask that question? Should it just be simply, do you not feel you are getting enough value? And then should there be any follow ups to that like maybe so they can find out in what area they don't feel they are receiving value?"

Chestin: "You probably wouldn't need to ask if they're getting enough 'value', but simply asking them why they're leaving should give plenty of insight. If they say they're leaving because they found someone cheaper, that basically means they didn't feel as if they were getting enough value.

Value can be defined as what your customer gets for the price they pay. So it stands to reason that if they're leaving for someone that offers it cheaper, they're not getting enough value.

If that is indeed the case, it's time to examine the way you're positioning your service. It might also indicate a need to better educate your customers on your services and why you are a better choice than the neighborhood low ball scrub.

But again, you'll never know why they're leaving unless you ask the question."

Gman: "I think that I'm offering my services too cheap for the amount of work that I'm doing for all my clients. If I'm there I am doing an extra small job for every client to improve their yard. And nine out of ten time I'm not charging anything. I was talking to another lawn care business owner, and he was telling me that I'm charging way too low. He would charge alot more then what I'm changing for the average lawn."

Troy: "Perhaps you just have the wrong type of customers and it has nothing to do with you. Perhaps because of how low your price is you are attracting the price shoppers.

Raise up your price and don't be disappointed that when customers tell you that you're too much. Don't expect to land every single account. If you do land every account, then "yes" your prices are definitely too low."

Steve: "I agree with Troy. If you were to raise your prices, you may tend to attract a different clientele. This would be a customer base who has no problem paying for services rendered and extra work when it is done."

Gman: "Thanks for the info it will help me. I will try to raise my price."

How to pre-screen customers when they call.

The previous question led to a great follow up question. If you are trying to get rid of low paying customers or customers that call looking for the lowest price, is there some way to pre-screen or pre-qualify them before you actually go out to visit them and give them a lawn care estimate?

Gman: "I should have a pre-screening list when I talk to the customers. Any help with that maybe 3 or 4 questions and which will the best one??"

Troy: "Let me throw you an example of different phone conservations that you might have with customers and in the conversations I am going to have what you SHOULD say and do. C=Customer and G=You

> **Situation 1:**
> G: This is Gman lawn care how may I help you.
>
> C: I am looking for someone to cut my lawn
>
> G: Are you looking for a one cut or seasonal service?
>
> C: I am just looking for a one time cut while my mower is serviced.

G: Well, I am sorry, we do not offer one time cuts. Sorry I couldn't help you.

Conclusion: Do not take on one time mowers. You will gain nothing from it in the long run. All they want is a cheap fix, not a long term solution

Situation 2:
G: Hello, this is gman lawn service how may I help you

C: How much would it be to mow my lawn?

G: Well, I would have to come out and look at the property first to determine your price.

C: Can't you give me a ballpark over the phone

G: No, Sorry I can not.

Conclusion: Do not take on a customer that wants an estimate over the phone. Now if they ask you that they would like you to come over and give them an estimate, then that is a different story.

Situation 3:
G: Hello, this is gman lawn service, how may I help you?

C: I would like an estimate for lawn maintenance.

G: Now this is for the entire season, correct?

C: Yes

G: Great. I will just take down your address so I can meet with you for the estimate and to talk about the contract

C: Contract? I am not signing a contract.

G: I am sorry, but all lawn maintenance accounts are required to sign a contract.

C: Forget it then

Conclusion: Why would they want to refuse to sign a contract? More than likely they probably would not be a good customer that would try to stiff you out of money.

Situation 4:
G: Hello, this is gman lawn service, how many I help you?

C: I need an estimate for lawn maintenance.

G: Not a problem, I would be more than happy to give you an estimate for seasonal weekly mowing.

C: No, I just need it mowed every 2 weeks.

G: I am sorry, but we only offer weekly mowing services.

Conclusion: This weeds out any bi-weekly customers lawns that may get super tall and super thick in which you would waste time and money on in the long run

So these are some examples that I have given you for when someone calls on the phone asking for an estimate."

To take part in this discussion further visit the post here

http://www.gophergraphics.com/forum/cgi-bin/ikonboard.cgi?
act=ST;f=8;t=4882

Using high fuel prices to attract new customers.

Normally you would think that higher gas prices would equate with having less clients, well in this discussion we will learn how you can take a bad situation and turn it into a win for you.

Tom: "With the rise of fuel, here is an idea. On your routes that have dead spots, print up a flyer for the neighborhood that could read something like: "Has your current lawn care company tried to impose a fuel surcharge, or have they told you they quit because they can't afford the gas - keep our number handy, Were local!"

With some real effort - this could be a way to get your name out after the season rush has ended. We get calls from "dropped customers" and they explain that the LCO wants more money because of travel."

Steve: "Those are some brilliant ideas. I hope others are reading this and paying attention. Have you tried it yet? Have you heard any feedback from this?"

Tom: "I have tried this and yes, feedback is great! I can understand hiding a fuel charge in the "per cost/cut" but you cant put a surcharge in a customers face and expect them to pay it! They don't own your truck or equipment and YOU, the Lawn Care Operator, need to find a way to offset the rise in fuel. One customer told me that her LCO wanted $6.00 more per cut for a fuel increase. I asked her if she plans to pay for their insurance increase too.

Another LCO flat out told a customer that they won't honor her agreement because demand for their company in her area was flat. Too bad for them - these are the 500K + homes that don't bat an eye at price. Johnny on the spot gets the work!"

If you would like to download this free flyer or join the discussion further, visit

http://www.gophergraphics.com/forum/cgi-bin/ikonboard.cgi?
act=ST;f=8;t=4919

GopherHaul 11

Overview of GopherHaul
Episode 11

Original Air Date: July 5, 2007

In this episode we discussed.
- Help a veteran marketing campaign.
- The bikini lawn care option.
- Flyer distribution methods.
- Business advice.
- GopherHaul 11 business book of the month.

Help a Veteran marketing campaign.

In honor of Armed Forces Day we asked our viewers to reach out to your community and see if there is a (military veteran or currently active) resident you can assist. Do something nice for them by helping out in their yard, take some pictures, and show us what you did. Out of the photos we will pick an lco who went above and beyond to help out a member of the military and we will send them (2 magnets 12x24...2-4 colors for their truck or trailer compliments of Tony From AMW-Graphics.com).

Also we have a professionally produced lawn care business program consisting of Business Tools, Manuals, Start-Up Guidance, Forms, Bidding and Estimating Tutorials, Estimating Calculators, Training Videos and much more designed to help you operate a successful Lawn Care Business, compliments of our friend Keith from summer101.com.

The winner of our contest was Lee of Tiger Time Lawn Care. Lee assisted Ed, a widower and a WWII veteran. Ed served three years in the military. He is no longer able to work on his yard now. Lee cut Ed's lawn and has redone his flower bed to give the yard more curb appeal!

Lee: "Being a retired vet myself I know the importance of helping them out. I have two others that I could have posted but thought Mr. Ed's was the best."

Check out the pictures Lee submitted for this contest here.

http://www.gophergraphics.com/forum/cgi-bin/ikonboard.cgi?
act=ST;f=1;t=5039;

Keep this idea in mind when you are looking for ways to help your community and get media attention for doing it.

Chadio: "I do this for a young woman in our community. It is only one. My father, grandfather, and uncles are veteran's who served overseas. When I left that job she was holding her daughter. As a father of two, I looked at my son, 2, who was with me and I felt good. I would hope someone would help my family while I was in harms way."

Lawncareinnovations: "A local news station called me today wanting to do a report on me because I posted an add on craigslist to help out local troops. I would cut there lawn of deployed troops for free! WOW What do you think should I do it or not?"

Steve: "Yes. Absolutely!

This is all about brand building! The more you build the brand of Lawn Care Innovations, the bigger you will grow.

Make sure you let them know about your military background and that you know how difficult deployment can be on a family. The more they know, the better the human story and the better it will connect with the viewers."

When you are building your business and are looking for ways to reach out to your community, you can either leverage your time or leverage your money. You can buy ads in papers or you can perform good will services such as the ones discussed here and then turn them into human stories which hopefully will be reported on in your local news. Also don't forget to make mention of your good deeds in your marketing material such as your website.

If you don't have many Veterans in your area, you can always offer to clean up a local park, or roadway. Help an elderly member of your community with a yard cleanup. Or anything else that takes advantage and shows off your abilities as well as brings attention to your business.

Do good deeds and then let everyone know about the good deeds you do! Send out press releases so the media knows what you are up to.

The bikini lawn care option.

In June of 2007, Lee was just starting up his new lawn care company and was looking for some ideas to really break out. He wanted to get his lawn care business going and he really hit on an idea that became fuel for an international marketing frenzy.

I wanted to take you back a little to how it got started.

Lee: "I have built a website for my company. I would like some of you, in the know, to give me some feedback on the site. Hey for team gopher check out the about us page along with the specials page.

*** Specials ***

Bikini Cut?

We have a staff of young ladies that will provide you with a grand pleasure for DAD or someone special. The ladies will arrive and perform lawn work in bikinis. This is a great deal for those that do not want to do the lawn but enjoy watching our ladies work. Call today to schedule your cut for Father's Day.

Call for more information!"

Steve: "WOW!

Lee are you really doing this?

If so, it has huge potential for media coverage. Take pictures and video. It would be a huge selling point and then put them on your website!

Maybe have them in tiger print bikinis or shorts!

Then get some posters made with them on it standing on grass saying something like "The Bikini Lawn Care Team." I bet you could sell them on your site as well or have them sold at the time of the lawn service. It could bump up the sale by another $10?

Tell us more about this plan!"

Lee: "Yes, We are doing it. It has started off slow but is picking up steam. I have attempted to order the tiger bikinis but can only get leopard and camo. We are still looking. I have two ladies doing it right now and I have bumped the price for the service. The funny part about it is that I have people coming out of the wood work wanting to work for me now. If this continues I will have a second crew soon."

You can join the discussion here

http://www.gophergraphics.com/forum/cgi-bin/ikonboard.cgi?act=ST;f=6;t=5045

In another post we continued this discussion.

Steve: "It's all an experiment. Sometimes something like this can help propel your name and brand out to more people then you could normally reach. You could always discontinue the service if it becomes too much of a hassle.

But here as we are talking about it, I am sure others in Lee's neighborhood will be talking too. That word of mouth buzz is invaluable."

Lee: "This is a fun thing that does draw a lot of attention. I am really hoping that I get a few calls for a father's day bikini cut. I think that is where I will draw the most attention.

Word of mouth is the best advertising that a company can get. Even if it is a little dicey."

Steve: "Lee have you gotten in touch with any of the newspapers yet? Or do you want to?"

Lee: "NO I am not sure I want the media coverage on this. It could be fun but I am just not sure of it. I have been contacted by several for the service."

Steve: "Oh. Well keep us posted as you go to let us know how things go with this. I think it is a great business experiment."

Lee: "It Happened! Rock 103 called today and asked about the bikini cut. I was floored. They put me on live radio and talked about it and the cost and a lot of good marketing stuff came out. I am not sure as to how they found out but in a way I am glad they did. They would like to do a promo with me and My Tiger Time team. I pray this is the start of something big and good for my business. I will try to keep you informed."

Steve: "That is great news! You know, maybe you should do some kind of contest with them. Give away a bikini lawn care cut to a listener of the radio station. I bet they would love that!"

Lee: "Yea that is the plan right now. We will give one away to a listener that can identify my rig. Well another good thing happened. The TV station affiliated with the radio station is doing a news event with us Thursday morning at 9:30. My team is getting pumped. I just keep thinking that all this is too good to be true. I will take pictures and post them.

The Camera Crew had a great time along with our team. It will air tomorrow morning at 8:30 AM on Fox News 13 here in Memphis."

Steve: "Have you heard much feedback from all of this? "

Lee: "We have gotten some great responses to the radio time we got. I may have to hire some more people. A local contractor contacted me about his 100 plus homes. Things could really be looking up. I know if I get the contract I will have to get more equipment."

Steve: "Lee, you are really blowing me away Great work! "

Lee: "Tom Dees from Fox News called and said that the clip is being picked up nationally. Good god! What have I done."

Steve: "OMG Lee that is awesome publicity!

Can you talk to them and see if you can get a copy of the video ? I bet they will send one to you or you could pick it up.

Once you get that, you could put it on your site. You could have a press area on your site to show off all the press coverage you get.

Some other things you should consider. Get your truck painted now in the tiger design. Then get a local professional photographer to stage some photos with the girls and the mowers and your truck once painted. You could use those pictures for postcards, your website and posters that you could sell on your site or sell to the customer for an additional fee when they sign up for your service.

You should do some other promos now too. Contact local businesses and have a promotion time set for the tiger time bikini girls to show up with the mowers and they could sign posters as giveaways. You could do this at sandwich shops, car dealerships, mower shops or other places that need to draw attention to themselves. You could charge a fee to be there with your staff. You could have them wear the tiger print bikinis too. Even if you have to hand make them.

This could get even bigger for you!

How about offering a service where they deliver flowers or even food?

Brainstorm and run with this idea!"

Lee: "Here we go again. This just continues to blow my mind. TV 5 will be doing a story on us today at 14:00 local time.
I will let you know the results.
P.S. I have gotten 10 new clients as a result. Funny thing is 8 of them are women. LOL."

Steve: "That is great!"

Lee: "Well it has taken off. I have had calls from all over the mid-south area. Some have been negative but most have been positive. We were on again last night with NBC channel 5. I had a call from a young lady wanting a job. LOL

Thanks Gopher you started this for me and the free advertising has been great and mostly positive.

The funny thing is most don't want the bikini cut but weekly lawn service. It is great."

Steve: "Lee did you see the article about you on Channel 5 wmctv? "

Lee: "Yes, I saw it. It was fun to do. We got a call this morning from Good Morning America. I am not sure what will happen with that one. National attention. I have a interview with a radio station in Kansas tomorrow morning and I got an email from Iowa to do another one. This is just unbelievable."

Steve: "HAHAHAHHAHA. That's amazing! What did the people from Good Morning America have to say to you?"

Lee: "They wanted to do an interview with me about marketing the bikini cut. I want you guys to know that I have mention you in every interview that I have done to date. It has gotten no air time but it is being said. It is so funny. I just keep being amazed at all of this."

Steve: "Maybe it's time to think about expanding! Franchise out the idea."

Lee: "I like it. I have had three radio interviews this morning. Iowa, Illinois and Arkansas. Every one asked me if I would do this very thing. I think I will work on it today and submit it to a lawyer for review. Iowa was more than interested funny."

At this point Lee's story went international and it was as if the genie was now out of the bottle. From initial idea to international news phenomenon, this all happened in less than a couple of weeks.

Billz: "I haven't been on here for weeks, so I didnt see the stories, until I heard about you on Paul Harvey!! LOL
I almost fell over, great job. I think you should take Gophers ideas on the ideas to cash in on your fame and make some money if possible!"

Lee: "This thing has gone a lot further than I thought. I now have a weekly contract with a radio station here to perform a bikini cut for free radio air time. If this is not becoming crazy I do not know what is. I am sure the novelty will die down soon.

Are you Kidding ME Paul Harvey?

This has become crazy. I would have never in my life time imagined this getting this big. I have lawyers calling, marketing people calling. I have been doing up to 6 radio interviews a day all over the place. CNN Radio is doing one today.

Good Morning America has called and wants to do something possible this week.

We are scheduled to be on Fox and Friends in the morning. I am looking forward to doing this. Can be fun. Can anyone think of this happening. I could have never imagined.

I think it will be live in studio. They wanted to come and pick me up and take me to the Memphis studio. I am getting ready right now and I have a phone interview with Boston Radio station to do in about 5 minutes. I will be on later this afternoon to find out what you thought.
I posted part of the new website thank you. I will finish it later.
I have cleaned up my email it is crazy the attention and emails I have gotten. Thank you guys."

Steve: "I watched Fox and friends. I must have missed the part when you were on but I did catch them talking about you later and they said they had tons of emails coming in about your service. Then they said they were going to do a follow up in the near future. How was the whole experience of being on the show?"

Lee: "I have gotten so much attention from all over. I did a radio interview last night in New Zealand. WMC5 want to do a follow up tomorrow. I did over 28 radio interviews yesterday alone and I have had two this morning. But, I have to say that with all the attention what make this all special to me is my friend on this forum are the best. You have provided me with the ideas and extra assistance when I needed it the most. All of you here are just great people. I have talked about this site and where the ideas all started from to just about every radio station and TV spot that I have gotten."

Keith: "How about this as an idea: You can travel to certain mower dealer locations with a couple of your tiger striped bikini-clad lovelies as promotional events. Have the girls show off the mowers to potential purchasers. Make sure the girls are well versed with all the technical aspects of the mowers and that they can really sell the machine. Make a mower the official mower of Tiger Time and use only their equipment.

Our local radio stations do "remotes" where they travel to locations and do a day's worth of promotion. You can work hand-in-hand with the local media to make sure your client (the local mower dealer) gets the most bang for his advertising dollar.

This idea can seriously keep you busy full time as there are hundreds of mower dealers and distributors around the country.

LOTS of business aspects to think about at this point."

Lee: "I think that is a killer idea. I am going to get in touch with our dealer here today and see if we can set up a promotional for next week. I will give the girls an education on the mowers and hope to make a difference.
I am at a point that I need some advice and legal assistance. I have had two production companies contact me about a reality show documentary, and a TV show spot in Atlanta. I do not know if it will happen but I have appointments next week about it.
Does anyone know a good lawyer that will help me with this?"

Who would have thought all this media attention would come over the simple concept of offering a bikini lawn care cut service as a promotion for Father's Day. I think one of the great lessons we can learn from this experience is that when an idea hits, sometimes it reaches out and can grow really fast. You have to be ready to jump on it or it will pass you by. I was really happy to see how much media exposure Lee got from all this. Don't be afraid to experiment with your marketing. You never know when your next idea will take off.

If you are interested in joining this discussion visit the post here

http://www.gophergraphics.com/forum/cgi-bin/ikonboard.cgi?
act=ST;f=4;t=5058

Lawn care business flyer distribution methods.

How often are you trying to come up with a way to drive through your neighborhood and distribute your lawn care business flyers as fast as possible? Have you come up with some crazy ideas on how to do it? Well, we have seen the best way to do it is usually the most time consuming. That is going door to door and meeting people as you hand out your flyers. If you are not going to do that and you don't want to mail your flyers, please whatever you do, don't do this.

A post on the Gopher Lawn Care Business forum showed a flyer that was thrown from a passing truck. It is enclosed in a sandwich bag and weighted down with some small stones. When we were talking about this on the forum, the point that came up is how mad it makes people. Homeowners consider this littering and not very earth friendly. If you get your potential customers mad at you, they are not going to call you for service.

Chestin from lawncaremarketingmagic.com: "While some might think this method is 'creative' and a way to stand out, it rarely leaves that impression. Successful marketing comes down to being a problem solver for people.

Unfortunately for this method, it makes anyone that uses it a bigger problem! Remember, you want to be a 'welcome guest', NOT an 'annoying pest'!"

Troy: "Yup, that is totally true. I would hate to wake up every week to a bag of rocks in my driveway."

Brandon: "I would be pissed if I found this in my driveway. Bad, Bad way to promote your business."

If you insist on throwing flyers out of your truck as you drive down the street how about stapling a small bag of grass seed to it? It's a unique marketing concept and the grass seed is a free gift from you to help the homeowner grow grass on bare spots.

If you would like to join this discussion visit

http://www.gophergraphics.com/forum/cgi-bin/ikonboard.cgi?
act=ST;f=8;t=5164

or our blog at http://lawnchat.com/?p=31

Darrin writes in for lawn care business advice.

Our friend Darrin contacted us and asked for help with his lawn care business.

Darrin: "In your GopherHaul show you said "If your business could use a GopherHaul, please contact us." so, I'm contacting you. I have seen your free flyers and such on your web site/forum. I have been in the business part time since 2005. I made my own flyers based on what I saw on those web sites. The first year I had 8 customers, The second year, I had problems with my truck and got a late start, then my 36" w/b mower broke and I didn't have the $400 for the part. I had 3 customers and only a 21" mower so I stopped advertising. I got a new (used) 48" w/b for free (cost me $55.33 in parts and about 8 hours to get it going) in July and did some more advertising. Got 1 call, didn't get the job.
This year I spent $3,300 on new equipment and repairs and advertising. Put out about 1500 flyers so far this year (I'll include them) and only got about 3 calls. I really need help BUT, I don't think I can afford it. Anything you guys can do would be greatly appreciated.

My "free lawn service" flyer was put out once, about 200 of them in one area, I got 2 calls, no jobs. Another coupon flyer was put out in another area at about 100, no calls. A third flyer design has been put out at about 1000 houses, 1 call. As you can see by the numbers, something is wrong, VERY wrong. I did not expect any jobs out of the flyers but, more than 2 calls would have been nice.

Thanks in advance"

Steve: "Here is my take. First off I really like what you are doing. I think your flyers are creative and being creative is a good thing.

Since you said you aren't getting a good response, I think I would get rid of the need for having to sign a contract. That might be scaring people away. I would also suggest using our free flyer "make the switch" we have in our flyer section.

Above and beyond all that. What else are you doing for networking? Are you handing out business cards to everyone you know? Are you talking with your neighbors? What's their response to your desire to service their lawns?

Are you using community bulletin boards in local stores?

Are you doing anything to get media attention in your area? Performing good deeds to others is a great way to accomplish this.

Do you have truck or trailer signs?

When you are distributing your flyers are you knocking on doors and meeting people? This is very important."

Brandon: "I was curious about something. When you send out the flyers, are you mailing them, dropping them on doorsteps, or something else. In my experience, knocking on doors and speaking to the people that answer can get you a lot further. I knocked on about 200 doors and left business cards with the people that answered, I left a business card at the door if no one answered. Of the 200 doors I knocked on, I got about 10 customers. It took about 2 weeks for all the calls to come in. It worked great for me. Hope this helps for you."

Darrin: "I am putting cards and/or flyers on community bulletin boards, cards in any business in the area that allows it, handing out multiple business cards to anyone I talk to. I also have a policy on business cards.... once I take it out of my wallet, pocket, whatever, I am not allowed to put it back. My truck is lettered. I am a volunteer EMT with the local ambulance corps but the policy there is that you can not profit from it at all. I have a green light on my truck so those that are aware of what that is used for, know that I am a volunteer. I only put must sign up, on the free mowing flyer, to ensure that I keep the customer longer than 5 weeks.

I put flyers on doors and talk to people who are around when I do that. I haven't actually knocked on doors. I am not busy this weekend so I will probably start that Saturday."

Steve: "Utilize all your talents and skills to help promote your business. You can use the fact you are a volunteer EMT in your marketing! Have you considered when you are treating your patients, if you see a certain patient really needs help, you could go back and clean up their yard for them. This would be a great media story. "Local EMT and lawn care business owner volunteers to assist a neighbor."

Use this connection in your marketing. Let people in your community know you are a volunteer. I would really consider including this information in your flyers as well. We have done this before with volunteer firefighters.

Maybe do some kind of community clean up of a public area? Have everyone meet up at the squad house. Have the local paper there to take pictures.

Maybe do some sort of fund drive. How many lawns can you cut in one day for free? Have people sign up to donate money to the squad. Maybe like a walk-a-thon where people donate based on how many miles they walk. You could go around asking people if they would donate to the squad and have others help you get more donations and people to sign up for you to cut their lawn. Maybe do this over a weekend.

People could donate $.25 or $.50 per lawn or whatever? Get the newspaper involved. This would be great promotion for you and a fund raiser for the squad. You would become a local hero!

You should always be asking yourself how can I leverage what I already do to get me more attention. The more attention you get, the more people will know about your business."

You can join in on this discussion by visiting the post here

http://www.gophergraphics.com/forum/cgi-bin/ikonboard.cgi?act=ST;f=8;t=5137

GopherHaul business book of the month.

This month's business book of the month for June 2007 is Metallica, This Monster Lives by Joe Berlinger.

As a business owner you should always be reading. It will help you and your business grow If you are a business owner you know that running a business can be a monster. This monster can take over your life and destroy everything. It can drive you to bankruptcy. You can lose your family. You can even lose your mind at times.

Which leads me to this book entitled "Metallica, This Monster Lives." This book gives you behind the scenes insight into the filming of Metallica's movie

"Some Kind Of Monster." This movie follows the band going through counseling and rehab for substance abuse after their bass player left in 2000. If you or someone you know is suffering from alcohol or drug abuse, please get help or get them help. It's tough enough trying to start and run your own business when you are healthy, if you are going to have any chance at all of finding success, you need to live a clean lifestyle.

In this book, it is really amazing to see that such a huge band with so many resources at their finger tips still deals with the same issues you and I deal with in our lives. I hope reading this book will leave you with this thought. Whatever is bothering you in your life, whatever difficulties you find yourself in whether they be substance abuse, financial issues, family issues or whatever, it is important for you to talk about them. Don't hold it in. It's important for you to talk. We all care about your well being.

If you haven't seen the movie, go out and rent it and read this book. I think you will find their journey to be inspirational.

To review the list of our previous GopherHaul business books of the month visit the post here.

http://www.gophergraphics.com/forum/cgi-bin/ikonboard.cgi?act=ST&f=1&t=792

GopherHaul 12

Overview of GopherHaul

Episode 12

Original Air Date: Aug. 5, 2007

In this episode we discussed.
- Don't put off starting your business.
- Updates on Lee and his bikini lawn care business.
- Lee explores franchising his lawn care business.
- GopherHaul 12 business book of the month.

Don't put off starting your business.

A few nights ago I got a phone call from a friend who's father had just died. He had worked for 35 years and dreamed of his retirement. When he retired he suffered a heart attack. Declining health followed for two years before his body finally gave out. He had dreams of going on a cruise to Alaska with his wife. He had dreams of fishing on his favorite lake. All these dreams are now gone. My message to you today is to make your dreams happen today. There may not be a tomorrow. Do it today. Enjoy your life today. Don't wait until you retire to have fun. Time is fleeting! Have fun and get your business started today!

Updates on Lee and his bikini lawn care business.

What's the big story of the month? Our friend Lee has really done it. He has managed to attract international media coverage for his lawn care business. I can't ever remember any lawn care business being able to get so much advertising for free. How did he do it? Bikinis.

He was mentioned in China, India, Australia. On the front page of CNN's site, on Fox & Friends, The New York Times and in a monologue for the Tonight Show with Jay Leno. Lee even gave our website a plug on Fox & Friends. If you have been active in our Gopher lawn care business forum, you probably already know how just 3 months ago, Lee left his job and decided to start a lawn care business. He posted on the Gopher lawn care business forum that he was looking for ways to attract customers. After going through a few ideas, he decided to go with the bikini lawn care service.

If you would like to join this discussion further, visit the post here

http://www.gophergraphics.com/forum/cgi-bin/ikonboard.cgi?act=ST;f=4;t=5058

Lee explores franchising his lawn care business.

Lee is now exploring franchising his lawn care business. If you are thinking about getting into the lawn care industry but have no idea how to get started, why not contact Lee and get started in one of his franchises. Lee was kind enough to allow us to give away 3 free franchises. Normally there would be an initial franchise fee of thousands of dollars to get started. If you contact Lee and mention you saw the free franchise deal you saw here on the GopherHaul show, you might be one of the lucky 3 who get a free franchise. Lee also wanted me to make note he would love to see people within a 200 miles radius of Memphis Tennessee contact him, but ultimately he will be choosing those applicants who are the most enthusiastic to make their franchise grow.

Steve: "How much they can expect to make with the franchise."

Lee: "I am giving away three at this point to the first three LCO's that would like to expand the business. After they are gone I have decided to go with 2000.00 buy in. 10% of gross revenue to the HQ. 3% of Gross revenue to be placed in a shared advertising account. The HQ will release monies as it is approved for advertising.

I am also going to provide a profit sharing for all managers of the company. I am getting calls daily for work. This is an opportunity that comes along once in a life time for some of us. I know it is for me."

If you would like to join this discussion further, visit the post here
http://www.gophergraphics.com/forum/cgi-bin/ikonboard.cgi?
act=ST;f=34;t=5351

What can we learn from the experience of GopherHauling Lee's lawn care business? If you are going to go into business, you need to stand out. Ask yourself, how do you differ from your competitors? What makes your business unique? What unique services can you offer that will generate media buzz about your company?

GopherHaul business book of the month.

The GopherHaul business book of the month is *L.L. Bean: The Making of an American Icon*. In this book we see how L.L.'s first attempt at getting into business was when he created a new hunting boot. He borrowed money from his family to send out ads to residents with hunting and fishing licenses. He was amazed to find that he sold 100 pairs of boots! Within a short period of time 90 boots were sent back because they were defective. This could have sunk his business and he might have never tried another business again. What did he do? He refunded those 90 sales and re-engineered his boot and tried again.

What's the business lesson we can learn from LL Bean? NEVER GIVE UP! If you fail at one attempt, review what happened and learn from your mistakes. Then give it another go and try to make it better the second time and the third time and the forth! Everyone makes mistakes but not everyone learns from their mistakes and tries again.

If you are going to be in business, don't ever give up.

GopherHaul 13

Overview of GopherHaul
Episode 13

Original Air Date: Sept. 5, 2007

In this episode we discussed.
- This episode marks GopherHaul's first full year in production.
- Lee's lawn care business gets new uniforms and is looking to expand.
- Do's and Don'ts of flyer distribution.
- How you can use an autodialer to market your lawn care business.
- How small landscaping jobs can bring in big profit margins.

GopherHaul celebrates it's 1st year anniversary.

This episode marks GopherHaul's first full year in production. One year sure has made a big difference. I thought it was fitting that to help celebrate our first year, we have had over 100,000 views! How fantastic is that.
I think it's wonderful we have been able to reach out to so many entrepreneurs. I know I personally have been having a blast and I thank you all for taking part in the show. This show has been getting a lot of really great attention.

We got a great review from Barbra of Home Business Wiz. She wrote "Have you ever checked YouTube for home business building videos? Granted there's a lot of junk, but there are also some gems. One that I like is GopherHaul. It's a show for lawn care operators and small business owners. Here's a sample episode with a good tutorial on how to make an effective lawn care business flyer."

Thank you Barbara for the positive review of our show, I do appreciate it.

Tiger Time Lawn Care gets new uniforms.

Next up. Lee's lawn care and his bikini lawn care service. I have been getting tons of responses asking about Lee and how his lawn care service has been going.

Well first off they are growing. Since our last show he has found some new business partners who want to help him expand his service into new areas. He also has finalized the new work uniforms.

You can see a picture of their new uniforms here
http://www.gophergraphics.com/forum/cgi-bin/ikonboard.cgi?
act=ST;f=34;t=5461

Brandon: "Have you thought about hiring a professional photographer to make the most out of the girls at work. Maybe setup a photo shoot where they are in action, but not really working so they aren't sweaty and stuff. The photographer can get them in the best poses and angles. Then you'll have something to put on the flyers that will really catch the attention of people. just an idea."

Lee: "Yes, It has been done already and I am waiting on the photos to get back to me. We had a bikini cut for a birthday party and we brought the photographer along. He has told me he got some great shots.
I am waiting to get them in."

Steve: "I like the photo concept! I think you should roll with what you got. I am also looking towards to seeing the other photos. Very good point Brandon. It is amazing what some good photos can really do to help convey your message.

I think your staff could probably help land a lot of new accounts through their myspace accounts. Some sort of incentive plan would probably really help push this. Maybe they could get a % of the job they sell through their myspace site as a referral."

Do's and Don'ts of flyer distribution.

When you are getting your lawn care business started, you might have an impulse to put your lawn care business flyers in mail boxes. Don't!

Ernest started off this discussion.

Ernest: "Last Tuesday I had a call and an offer to cut a lawn. The caller said that other lawn companies would say they would show up to look at the lawn and come give her a price. Then they would come back in a day to cut it but that would be the end of it. She called telling me that she found my flyer in some paper work on her computer desk and for some reason she kept it. The flyers do work!

So I gave her a day to look at the yard, told her I would come two days later and needless to say I showed up and I got the yard. She had another appointment with another company, but since I was the only one to show up when told her they would come, she choose me. This was my first lawn but I seemed to have pulled it off, for this is a weekly account now. I just hope I am charging enough to make a little $$. Wish me luck for more business."

Chris: "Keep pumping out those flyers. As most of the country is in a heat wave. Fri and Sat nights are good times to toss out flyers. I repeat neighborhoods about every 5 weeks. or so.

When people get out to mow on Sat morning, they find my flyer. Toss it in the garbage, start mowing, feel the heat... think to themselves. This sucks.. Then they dig it out of the trash and give me a call. I get at least one account for every 250 flyers I throw out."

LawnCareInnovation: "What flyer are you using?"

Ernest: "I am using the one free template that asks "Are you paying too much?" I looked at it this way, if I was the one who needed lawn work done that flyer would catch my attention."

Steve: "What has been the best way you have found so far to distribute your flyers? "

Ernest: "So far, I got this lawn by putting them in the mailbox. I figured so that when they check the mail they already have it in their hand. I want to distribute more flyers around that neighborhood, try to keep it in the same area so that fuel would not be a problem. I am looking for a bigger truck my S-10 is not really made for doing this kind of work, but it is great for now. For the fall I was thinking of fabricating a clean up special, don't know about prices yet. And for the winter I can not offer anything in the area of snow removal since it does not snow in Florida so I was thinking of offering to take decorations down during the holidays."

Steve: "Did you know that is illegal? Legally you can't put anything in the mail box. I think you might be better off putting them in doors or using door hanger. We hear quite often how the postmaster will call a lawn care operator for doing this and make them take all the flyers out. You can also be fined! Yikes!"

Ernest: "I knew it was illegal to tamper with the mail, but I did not know about putting anything in the mail box. It would be a good idea to stay away from any kind of fine. How would I go about getting the door hangers and would I be able to print theme out on my home printer?"

Steve: "There is door hanger template paper out there like this http://www.blanksandbags.com/

Or you could go with the magnetic business card concept and stick them to the doors.

Or, you could, use pre-printed post-it notes! Did you know you could get them pre-printed with your message on them? Then you stick them to the door as well."

Ernest: "I sure do like the post it idea. I like the concept of sticking it to the door, If you put in about the eye level your pretty much guaranteed that it would be seen. I have been looking at this lawn. the grass seems to be a little tall for a couple of weeks and I have not ever seen a lawn company there, I am thinking of actually knocking on the door and offer them a quote. Thanks, real excited about trying to get another account."

Steve: "Something interesting about seeing tall grass we have discussed many times in the forum is this. You would think initially that a home with tall grass would be a great candidate for a lawn care company, but there is probably a reason why the grass is tall. Mainly the inability to pay for lawn care service."

To join in on this discussion or read more, visit the Gopher Lawn Care Business Forum here.

http://www.gophergraphics.com/forum/cgi-bin/ikonboard.cgi?
act=ST;f=26;t=5437;st=10

Using an autodialer to promote your lawn care business?

For years before the federal government created the do not call list, telemarketing was the way the big lawn care businesses promoted their services.

In this episode we got a chance to meet Chris, who had just wrapped up his mortgage business and was going to use his autodialer to attract new lawn care business prospects.

Chris: "Hey guys, Well here's a short intro about myself...
I'm 26, have a beautiful wife, and 3 awesome kids 1,6,8. I had my own mortgage company for the last 5 yrs. It was awesome financially but I never got to see my family. So I shut it down in Feb. '07. Since then I have been spending 24/7 with my family. But now its time to get back to work. I love making my grass the best in the neighborhood and that obsession has turned into me wanting to have my own landscaping company. I really have a passion for it.

I know its mid season right now, but i would really like to start it now!!!! My brother just left for the army and will be back in November and i would love to have it up and running and have him become a business partner.

I am very familiar with direct mail and websites, but something I didn't see that worked in the mortgage industry is auto dialers...

So my question to you guys is... would an automated message work for getting new clients?

I have an 20 line autodialer or access to a service that would do 50,000 calls in 1hr.

It would leave a brief message under 30 secs. or a message that prompts them to press 1 to speak directly to me.

What do you guys think?"

Steve: "Is an auto-dialer legal? Is the list cross referenced with the federal do not call list?

If it was ok to use, I'd try it out. Why not? Have a quick sales pitch and then ask the listener to leave their address if they would like a free estimate and maybe some other teaser.

Let us know if you try it."

Chris: "Actually all my leads I buy are scrubbed for me for the state and federal do not call list and auto dialers are illegal if you were to dial phone numbers in order.
555-1234
555-1235
555-1236 etc...

I always got awesome response in the mortgage world and cant wait to put something together for the landscaping world!!!

I started to record a message for my auto dialing campaign, does anyone have a suggestion on a message??

It needs to be max 30 sec. but the shorter the better because I can get more calls out.

> **Ex.** Hi this is My Landscaping Company. we are currently offering free estimates for mowing, trimming, and edging. Press 1 now to schedule your quote.. pause we also offer a referral program, refer 1 customer get your lawn cut for free 1 time and if you refer 10 customers you get a fall clean up valued at $250. press 1 now pause For your free estimate or referral bonus. press 1 now pause please press 2 to be removed from our list

what do you think??"

Chestin from Lawncaremarketingmagic.com : "I know this is too late to include this in the message, but maybe you can keep it in mind for next time.

I would have made a stronger offer. Instead of just offering free estimates (every one does those these days), I would have offered a free '21 point lawn care analysis' with an opportunity to get XX% off.

Now, what's the 21 point analysis? It's simply the free estimate except you have 21 different things (or some other relevant number) you check and then give recommendations on. It's really nothing more than your regular estimate, but by giving it a title it makes it sound much more valuable and people will be more interested to get it.

So, here's what I would've said in the message:

> "Hi, this is Chestin from Your Landscaping Company. I wanted to call to let you know that for the next 2 weeks only we're offering our 21-point lawn care analysis for free. This thorough analysis will give you a detailed picture of the state of your lawn and provide you with several recommendations for making it the greenest, thickest lawn in the neighborhood.

To schedule your free, no obligation appointment, simply Press 1. If you'd prefer to not receive further notice of our special offers, simply Press 2.

Remember, we're only offering this no commitment 21 point analysis for the next 2 weeks so Press 1 to schedule your appointment now!"

There's a couple of key elements that were missing from the original message that I added to this version."

Steve: "Possibly offer a third option? Where you can sign up for a free lawn cut with an annual contract?"

CleanLawn: "Ok for those of us that don't know anything about this auto caller thing can you tell me how to find out more information on it? This is actually something I could do from anyone of my other two business' while there is down time.

I think this is a great idea and in such a large area, we could drum up a lot of new business."

Chestin: "Here are 3 different voice broadcast services that you could use:

- www.voiceshot.com
- www.protus.com
- www.callfire.com

They all have pretty easy online setups and their prices are reasonable. I've never used www.callfire.com, but they have the cheapest rates. $03.5/minute compared to $.05 to $.15/minute with others."

Cleanlawn: "Maybe it was just me but you said what the original post said again but you dressed it up. A free lawn estimate = everyone is doing that but a 21-point lawn analysis sounds like your getting the royal treatment when in fact it is the same exact thing.

You also gave the customers a timeline, which is 2 weeks. Without a timeline to me it sounds like this is something you do all the time but a trying to dress it up and sell it. Most people don't know that these services are offered all the time. They feel like your doing something special by the 21-point lawn analysis being done special for 2 weeks only. Frankly, I would be more likely to call someone selling the 21 point lawn analysis over the everyday I can do this estimate in my sleep because I do it so much.

Then giving the customer the knowledge of what they can or cannot do themselves to fix their lawns makes them feel like they have the power to choose to do it themselves or have a professional do it."

Chris offered us a follow up on his autodialer, a short time later.

Chris: "My autodialer is getting me 6 to 8 jobs per 3000 dials

I've been brokering out the lawn care jobs I can't do for 10% to a much bigger company close to me!"

Chestin: "Excellent use of technology! I imagine if you land 2, maybe even just 1 client it will have paid for itself. Good job.

Have you considered doing a follow-up message? Statistics show you'll get even more responses with a second message to the same list.

I'll be very interested to hear about your overall results."

If you'd like to read up more on Chris and his autodialer, here are some posts to read over.

http://www.gophergraphics.com/forum/cgi-bin/ikonboard.cgi?act=ST;f=1;t=5543

http://www.gophergraphics.com/forum/cgi-bin/ikonboard.cgi?act=ST;f=26;t=5287

http://www.gophergraphics.com/forum/cgi-bin/ikonboard.cgi?act=ST;f=8;t=5386

http://www.gophergraphics.com/forum/cgi-bin/ikonboard.cgi?
act=ST;f=8;t=5477

Small Jobs can bring big profits.

Are you offering small jobs? Troy is and he has been making some big profits because of it.

He wrote us to say a lot of the jobs he is getting are from current customers or just one time customers calling up for something simple. The last two days this is what he had done and the profit margins.

1. Pruned a vine 82% profit margin
2. Pruned an ornamental tree away from a homeowners roof 74% profit margin
3. Patched up and seeded a lawn where another lco spilled gas 87% profit margin
4. Replaced sprinkler heads 82% profit margin
5. Adjusted a sprinkler system 79% profit margin

He doesn't market these either, they just call up and ask. Most of these jobs only take him 15 to 20 mins to do, with a $54 minimum price for most of them. The longest job took him 1 1/4 hrs and that was adjusting the sprinkler system.

Troy said he has always provided these services in the past. But he totally changed around his pricing structure and pricing policy this year. No matter what, there is a minimum $54 charge and of course the rates have increased this year as well.

Troy advises other lawn care operators to be sure to always have a minimum charge set in place for each particular service. For example, most of his services, which do not include a power tool or equipment, are $54 per hour with a minimum $54 charge no matter what.

Also consider your turn around time? How fast can you get the product installed or service the property. If you are quicker than another company, then charge away. An example of this is the seeding that he did for one customer. A woman who called Troy had been waiting for over a month from her current lawn care operator to seed some patches in here lawn. She finally gave up and called Troy. Troy told her that he could take care of the problem within the next two days and he did. Even though it only took him about 20 minutes to do the job, he delivered a quality service with a fast response and charged a premium for it

Keep this idea in mind when you are trying to figure out how to make more profits.

GopherHaul 14

Overview of GopherHaul

Episode 14

Original Air Date: Oct. 2, 2007

In this episode we discussed.
- Making money with outdoor Halloween decorations.
- How to bid leaf clean up jobs.
- Free Halloween lawn care marketing material.

Making money with outdoor Halloween decorations.

If you are looking for ways to make more money this fall, consider letting your creativity flow and offer your customers outdoor Halloween and fall decorations. Mix pumpkins, gourds, hay and corn stalks to create a very festive looking residential yard or commercial property.

One of the great benefits of running the Gopher Lawn Care Business Forum and hosting the GopherHaul show, is that I get a chance to meet so many interesting and talented people.

In this episode, I talk about some of the amazingly creative outdoor Halloween decorations my friend Anthony from United Environment was able to construct for a local pizzeria. When Anthony first sent me the photos and showed me the video of what he was working on, I thought to myself, Anthony is so talented he will be moving on up anytime now to bigger and better things.

The pizzeria was converted into something out of a horror movie. Giant spiders were positioned on the side of the building and a guillotine was crafted from scratch. After watching all this I was not surprised to find out Anthony had gotten out of the lawn care business and started his own movie company. If you get online, do a search for his horror movie Ratred.

I am convinced one day we will be watching his movies on the big screens in theaters.

If you are interested in learning more about Anthony I was lucky enough to record a podcast with him. Check out my podcast link on the forum and you will see one of my earlier podcasts included an interview with him.

How to bid leaf clean up jobs.

Next up let's talk about how to bid on a leaf clean up job.

There are plenty of pitfalls when you get involved with fall yard clean ups.
I want to share with you a story posted on our forum by our friend Keith, owner of www.startalawncarebusiness.com

In his first year of owning a lawn care company. A new customer called to get an estimate for raking the yard and cleaning out gutters. He had several large trees in his yard. Although his yard was covered with leaves more than half of the leaves were still on his trees. Since he had a mulching area to keep me from having to haul off his leaves, I gave an estimate of $150. The customer did not want to spend that much and said to Keith if he would do it for $110, he could also cut the yard next year. The leaf job went well and Keith collected his money and went home. The next day the customer called to say that Keith had not raked all the leaves and that he needed to come back. Keith explained that the leaves in his yard had fallen after he had finished and that he was not responsible for those leaves. Not wanting to lose the business next year, Keith ultimately went back and did a quick touch up job which took an hour. Keith was then satisfied as it was a big yard and he would get to do his mowing work all the following year.

When Spring rolled around, Keith took his equipment to the customer's house and was told that someone else had already been contracted to mow the lawn for the season. Keith reminded the customer of the agreement they had and the client said that the other lawn care business was doing the job for $5 less than Keith's estimate.

WOW Can you imagine that!

Here are a few lessons Keith learned from this customer.

> 1) He did not have a signed agreement. You should be very careful about taking a customer's word they will let you do their lawn "next season" in return for a cheaper price today. If the agreement is verbal it is very easy for a customer to back out of the agreement.

> 2) Price each job as an individual effort. If a leaf job is worth $250 to you then bid it accordingly. Do not let the potential of other work influence your price significantly downward. That other work may never materialize.

> 3) Explain to the customer that leaves on the trees are not included in the price. Leaves continue to fall through the entire season. If you contract to do a leaf job, let the customer know that any leaf droppage that occurs after the job is done is not covered under the quoted price.

When Keith consults with new lawn care business owners, he often tells them that leaf pickup is very easy to under price. A job which looks like it should take less than 1 hour can often wind up taking 4 times that long.

This Autumn, when your phone starts ringing with new customers looking to get a great price on leaf management, take extra caution when giving estimates.

One of our friends and forum member Brandon, told us this cautionary tale as well.

Brandon: "When I started my business, I had a property management co. give them a bid on a leaf clean-up job. The yard had 3 large elms on it. I gave the bid of $150 and submitted it in writing. Well it was more than 2 weeks later when they had gotten back to me with the approval and I told them I will get right on it tomorrow. In that 2 weeks, at least 3 times as many leaves had fallen, which turned a 2 hour job into almost 5 hours. It was a nightmare, not to mention it had rained the few days before. It was awful. This year I am going to tell people the bid is good for 48 hours, and bid accordingly.

You might want to consider a 48 hour expiration on your bids as well."

Free Halloween lawn care marketing material.

To help you promote your outdoor fall decorations, we put together a bunch of free flyers and doorhangers you can download and edit to fit your needs. Here is one of them. Visit http://www.gophersoftware.com to download all our free lawn care marketing templates.

GopherHaul 15

Overview of GopherHaul

Episode 15

Original Air Date: Oct. 16, 2007

In this episode we discussed.
- How to overcome the difficulties of running a lawn care business as a single mom.
- Mower winterization service idea.
- Marketing tips for Halloween.

Running a lawn care business as a single mom?

On the forum, we all get a chance to meet many creative thinkers and business people. Both men and women are out there running their own businesses everyday. In this discussion we get a chance to help one of our forum members who runs her own business. Our friend Teresa joined us and she was in the midst of multitude of problems.

Teresa: "Here is a brief run down of the past 4 years. March 2003, started a lawn care business. Things went great till May 2005 when my husbands colon exploded and he almost died. November 2005 doctor said he could go back to work but he refused. There had always been verbal abuse in our marriage but I just ignored him. He decided he was going to do nothing but sit around and try to collect a check. The abuse went from just verbal to physical, mental and emotional. He also started bringing my children into it as well. The last straw was him throwing my 8 year old daughter into a wall. October of last year I had him removed from the house with a restraining order. A year has pass now and my children and I are still in therapy. Both of the children now 9 and 10 are diagnosed with post traumatic stress disorder due to domestic violence. Now here is my problem, for the past year my ex has done nothing but run his mouth about me and my business because he thought I should have sold it and split with him but the judge said no that is her job you cannot have any part of it. I have lost customers due to this and cannot get new ones in the immediate area because of him. There are several areas I would like to get into but I got what I have by word of mouth and I am not sure what the best move for me would be.

I do have 2 questions to any who want to answer.
1. How do you inexpensively introduce yourself to a new area? and
2. What does everyone else do during the winter months which are really only Dec., Jan., and Feb. for me.

Single mom, two children. Suggestions please."

Steve: "Welcome to our forum!

There are a couple things I can think of, depending on how into this you want to get.

First off, Halloween is coming and you have kids. Have you considered going out and trick or treating with them and handing out flyers as you do this? It would be a great way to reach out to new people and make a personal connection.

I also think you have a great story. It's great because others will be able to relate to you and they will want to see you succeed because you will then be a hero for single women, trying to do this all on your own.

I would consider putting together an article for your local paper, where you talk about this. The headline could read "Being a single mom and running your own business isn't easy." It could be a very inspiring story. Put together a press release and include a picture of you and your children. And talk about all the issues you face doing this on your own but how you are determined to succeed.

In fact, we could help you put this together right here on the forum and others could offer their views as well.

Doing something like this, really puts your story out there but it also takes a bad situation and makes it a positive one by harnessing it. Others will read the article and relate to you and want to hire you. They will be able to connect with you and your struggle.

What's your take on this?

You could also go out and do flyers and door hangers but I think this would be so much more powerful! "

Chestin from http://www.lawncaremarketingmagic.com: "Here's how I would tackle the issue of rebuilding your customer base.

First, has your ex completely burned any possible bridges with your customers? If there's even the smallest chance of salvaging a relationship, I'd send these customers a letter touching on the fact your business has been sabotaged but that it's going to benefit them. There's no need to go into the specifics, but let them know that you're willing to do whatever it takes to keep their business so you'll offer them a sizable discount or premium to stay with you.

If there's no chance of salvaging anything and you do have to start over, these are the steps I'd go through to rebuild your business:

1. Create a 'farm' or list of target prospects. If you're on a tight budget, the best thing to do is drive around and identify neighborhoods you want to target.
2. Create a flyer introducing your business and make them an incredible offer. Remember to include these critical elements in your flyer:

   - An attention grabbing headline.
   - Present them a valuable offer.
   - Create urgency with either a limited number available or deadline.
   - Tell them exactly how to respond.
   - Include 3rd party proof (Before/After photos, testimonials, etc.)
   - Provide risk reversal or something to remove any risk.

3. Walk these neighborhoods distributing the flyers and hand deliver as many as possible to a live person. Yes, it will take some time, but it's one of the most effective methods available on a limited budget

   Lastly, if you have any customers left, I'd send them a letter telling them you're trying to grow your business and that you need their help. Offer them a premium if they'll refer you to some of their friends or neighbors.

Another thing you could do would be to approach realtors, accountants, financial planners, or any other service business that services the same profile customer as you. Try to create some type of joint venture with them where they'll refer you to their clients in exchange for either you doing the same or you providing them service for a period of time.

These are all things you could do to quickly get your business back up and running.

Also, with respect to the press release Steve mentioned, I'd love to help out with putting one together for you so just drop me a PM and let me know how I can get in touch with you to discuss it."

Keith from http://www.startalawncarebusiness.com : "Some good responses above.

First off, congratulations on having the guts to keep striving with your lawn care business. I am sure you are going though a tough time. Keep going...this, too, shall pass.

I think mothers and single women will admire what you are doing. This might help you find a whole new customer base. What if women became your target customer?

Single women might really take to the idea of another woman handling their lawn care jobs. You will be less threatening and you can lend a sympathetic ear.

You could get started by going to your local women's crisis center. Speak with the directors to see if they know of women going through divorces, etc. who need help with upkeep of their yards. Maybe offer 5% off to customers who are referred by the crisis center.

Advertise at local women's functions. Our town hosts an annual 10K run for breast cancer awareness. Literally thousands upon thousands of runners take part in that race. You could become a sponsor to an organization such as this.

There are probably lots of women's support organizations that you could become affiliated with.

This next suggestion can really be big for you. Lots of government related contracts have stipulations that they actively encourage women owned and minority businesses to bid on their projects. Take advantage of any special considerations afforded you.

If you do decide to go after the women only marketplace, your logo can be more dainty than what a big sweaty guy would use. A pink back ground with a lawn mower and a pair of gardening gloves over the handle. You might be able to hire a partner and your tag line can be something like:

Lawn Care For Women By Women!

You can have customized pink paint jobs done on your commercial lawn equipment. Your truck or lawn care trailer can be painted pink too.

Forget about the trash talking that may or may not be going on behind your back. Set your sights forward. You have a great opportunity to have a really strong lawn care business."

Steve: "I am totally with Keith on this. Accentuate your uniqueness.

I LOVE the pink idea.

Slogan ideas: Lawn care with a woman's touch or your lawn care deserves a woman's touch.

Keep it short and simple and play up that your business is a woman owned business. Absolutely.

Another great thing you could do would be to offer yourself as a guest lecturer to women's groups to discuss running your own business and doing it as a single mom. This could be really big for you. First off, it's something you can do for free and you will be reaching out to other local women and potential customers.

Do one guest speaking position somewhere and more requests will follow."

Rhonda: "Well as a woman lawn care owner I am sorry I missed the beginning of this post but I have been down and out with a horrible cold.

I agree with everything the guys have said and I am just a baby when it comes to the lawn care business (started June 2007) but they are 100% on the money.

I am sorry about the divorce and the trash talking. I have been there and wow does it suck when kids are involved but you have to think of yourself and them. If he wants to trash talk then let him, you have great people on this forum that can and will help. If ever need someone to talk to I have been there and it was horrible but I am here and I am married again to a great guy. Keep your head up and follow the great advice here. I was really overwhelmed with how great everyone was in the suggestion and help offered. Ya'll are awesome!

I was curious by one of the posts regarding the government contracts and women owned businesses? Are these considered commercial contracts and how would someone else go about finding information on it?

Again, keep your head up and everything will work out great!"

S.P.: "Your situation caught my eye as I have close up and personal experience from having to investigate and arrest those that batter spouses and family members.

In addition to the ideas posted here about promoting your business, you should put an effort at shutting up the ex. If you have evidence that his bad mouthing has cost you business, time for legal action.

I think you should fight back as all he is trying to do is keep control over you any way he can. You can't let him win. When the time comes that he realizes he can't control you anymore, he will disappear off the radar screen.

Do not be afraid to seek out help from organizations that help out women escape domestic violence and enable them to strike out on their own. The resources are out there and want to see you succeed, as do all of us."

Rhonda: "Well I didn't want to get this personal but I want Teresa to know that there are other women out here trying to also make a go at it so she is not alone. Teresa I can tell you I know 250% where you are coming from. I post that I was married before. It was an extremely verbally abusive relationship. That I put up with for 5 years. I left the day after the relationship turned from verbal to abusive when I told my husband I wasn't taking anymore of his **** and he punched me in the face. I had to constantly face the women he was sleeping with and thought I was too stupid to even know about. I didn't have anything then. I didn't even have enough respect for myself of my child to leave until it was too late. I lost a lot from that relationship but for a long time I thought that was a normal relationship because that is what I grew up with from my stepfather and my mother. My stepfather was an alcoholic, slept around and even went so far as to molest his stepdaughters. You don't have to sit there shocked with mouthes hanging wide open or shaking off a tear. They aren't worth it and I am not the same person now that I was then. 10 years ago I wanted to start a lawn care and landscaping business. My family told me I couldn't do it, that I would never amount to anything in this world.

Since then I have left my family. My ex-husband and my mother, sisters, everything. I left them behind because of everything they did and didn't do to stop any of the #### they put us through. I am married again to an incredible person. He was the one who helped me leave that life behind. I have a beautiful home, and we were blessed with a son who is now 2 years old. His whole world is growing up so he can work at our business. Mommies business and cut grass and drive a big truck. They make it all worthwhile. Your children are your world and they are very strong. Then take more then most people will ever know. They see you being strong and surviving. Making more and more of yourself everyday. Your an incredible role model for them. Don't ever worry about your husband and his unkind words. They cannot say nice things because they have put themselves in such a world of #### they do not know how to be nice or say nice things. The customers that listen to your husband and believe the foolishness that comes out of his mouth are not people you want in your customer base. Scratch them off the list and move forward.

Its already been one year for you. One year and many many more to come. Focus on the positive. You created a great business and these guys are awesome and will help you find even more greatness in your business. I just started my business at the beginning of June 2007. I had maybe 4 residential accounts and I just signed last month for nine residential property contract. Its nothing to you all who are veterans compared to people like me but it was huge for me. Even after 8 years of leaving that horrible life behind me I need things like 9 residential properties at once to make me realize I am doing something right. I wish I had not listened to my family and started this 10 years ago but I didn't. I read what these gentlemen suggest. Everything I can. I am trying to work a lot of what they are telling you into my business because like you, I know what I have and I just want the rest of the world to know how great it is too.

Right now I am working on landscaping packages that I am going to push in the spring. I think its a good idea and will work with a lot of hard work. I also think trying to get in with realtors. I think if they would purchase small contracts for homes that sell it would help push great businesses like ours and the gentleman on here but convincing them of that isn't so easy. I also think pushing gift certificates at Christmas time for lawn care services would rock! But that won't likely happen till next year for me.

I want to create a webpage but everything takes time and money. I buy things as I can. I guess what I am saying is stick with it and never give up your dreams and it will all fall into place. The woman's touch thing for lawn care is great and would work well considering everything you have been through and you can benefit from it. Hang in there it gets better. "

Teresa: "Thank you very much for sharing your story with me. You are right it is hard to pick up and move on. I have been more inspired this week than I have been in a long time. Right now I need to focus on two things MY CHILDREN and promoting the heck out of MY BUSINESS. Hopefully one day like you I will find a wonderful man who will want to share life with me. There is one really interested, I can't go there yet. I need to be independent and stand on my own two feet for awhile."

Rhonda: "I agree 100% with you. You need to show yourself how strong you really are by standing on your own two feet. Your two beautiful children will be a source that you will use to find strength for yourself when you least expect to find it but it will be there. Your children, your lawn care business and yourself will all be all right. You are a lot stronger then you think. You came forward and shared with all of us. That is strength. Take up these wonderful guys on the webpage and help with marketing ideas, newspaper articles, everything and keep your eyes out for more ideas in these forums. Everyone has ideas and we all share them and just because one idea might not work for you another one might.

You're welcome to try to push any idea I throw out in any thread in these forums and I love feedback. It's what helps me make great decisions for my lawn care and landscaping business. It is only a couple months old but I look forward to the day when I can look back and see how much I have grown and how much even in a few months everyone has helped me.

If you ever just need to talk I am a great listener and I have been there before. If I can help, I will. Whether you know it yet or not, your very strong and independent and your children have a great role model to look up to. You deserve a big pat on the back hun, your doing great! "

I really thought this was a touching and inspiring discussion and I am so glad it was brought up so we could all discuss it. We all go through ups and downs in our life. I hope by reading this forum discussion it inspires you to push forwards no matter what situation you find yourself in.

Mower winterization services idea.

In the winter time when the lawn care business slows down, what are you planning on doing? Our friend Patrick came up with a great idea I wanted to share with you.

Patrick: "Here's an idea me and my partner have been considering as well...

So we have a LOT of people around our area that LOVE to get out and do their own yard work. That's fine. All we have to do is send out a flyer saying we will come by their house in the fall and winter and SERVICE THEIR EQUIPMENT for them. That way, when they get ready to fire up the mowers in early spring, all they need to do is connect the battery and fire them up! They call us with the equipment list they want serviced (including the models) and we'll get the parts, bring the parts and tools to their house, sharpen the blades, change the oil, etc etc etc...

What do you think?"

Steve: "That is an awesome idea! And why not! What would you suggest charging? Are there other services you would add?"

Patrick: "I guess it depends on if you're providing the supplies (oil, filter, etc) or not. If THEY provide the supplies, then yeah, I would say about $30-40... if you're providing it, then I would say add in the cost for the supplies.

Don't forget, you can also...

...inspect tires and inflate to proper pressure (if necessary)...
...sharpen hedge trimmer blades (manual trimmers)...
...check/change spark plugs on weed eaters and blowers... "

Peter: "Thats an awesome flyer and I have little knowledge on servicing a mower. I have a small engine mechanic that works on all my small engine equip. But this could help out someone that has a lot of skills in small engine repairs. "

Patrick: "You don't have to have a ton of knowledge about small engine repairs. Just change the oil and filter, change the air filter, and maybe clean it up a little.

I'm sure you could find some online resources with enough information to get you through. As we were talking about in another post... "Fake it till you make it!""

Rob: "If you're thinking about doing a winterization service for peoples mowers there's more you need to do than just change the filters and oil. One very important thing that needs to be done so it will start in the spring is making sure that all the gas is out of the carb and drain it out of the tank. Or use a fuel stabilizer in the tank and run it so it gets into the carb. Easiest way is just to run it out of gas. Otherwise the gas will start to turn to a varnish and gum up the carb jets and float. I did this with a chain saw I had and it started right up with fresh gas after 2 years of sitting. I used to be a small engine mechanic about 5 years ago. I forgot some of it but I still remember the basics. Sharpening the blades is easy once you do it a few times. Make sure you have a balancer with you."

Patrick: "I have heard in almost everything I have read to empty the gas tank and leave it empty. I would offer this for thought: I read in one particular set of instructions to do just the opposite... fill the gas tank to the maximum... add a conditioner to help prolong the life of the fuel and also keep it from freezing (not sure if gas even freezes). This way, the inside of your tank doesn't rust from any condensation that may occur. Nothing worse than trying to start your mower and immediately clogging your new, clean fuel filter.

I guess this also depends on what state you live in... how cold it gets and where your mowers are kept would play a role on my decision... like I live in Georgia... it doesn't get TOO cold here, so I'm not worried about the gas freezing (never has before). Plus, I've never drained the tanks before.

...and whether your gas tank is metal or plastic. My rider has a plastic tank, but my push mowers have metal ones... naturally, plastic doesn't rust. I guess it's just as easy to leave gas in a tank as it would be to leave it in a gas can. "

If you would like to experiment with this service in the winter time, we put together a free flyer you can download and edit. Visit the Gopher Lawn Care Forum and click on the free flyer section or visit this discussion and join in.

http://www.gophergraphics.com/forum/cgi-bin/ikonboard.cgi?act=ST;f=26;t=5668;st=50

Halloween marketing ideas.

Rodman made a great find and started a discussion on how the M&M's website offers custom printed M&M's. You can also get them with your business logo on them. So why not consider getting some custom printed M&M's this year that promote your lawn care business name and phone number and hand them out to all the kids that visit your home.

Join this discussion at the Gopher Lawn Care Business Forum here.

http://www.gophergraphics.com/forum/cgi-bin/ikonboard.cgi?act=ST;f=17;t=5916

GopherHaul 16

Overview of GopherHaul
Episode 16

Original Air Date: Oct. 30, 2007

In this episode we discussed.
- New free job bid proposal form.
- Search engine optimization techniques.
- Why you shouldn't bid on huge jobs that are outside your scope.
- How to market lawn service to home sellers.

Job bid proposal form.

Rob made a post on the forum asking about bid proposal forms.

Rob: "When I want to submit a bid for a commercial account; is my bid sheet suppose to have some kind of format? I have my own using a template from Microsoft word that I made fit my needs. It works fine for me with my residential customers. But I don't think that it is something that I want to be using to give to a property manager or using to submit bids. It doesn't seem fit for that.

I'll try to put in up here so you can see it. Maybe it just needs to be modified a little. It's kind of small.

Can the people that have commercial accounts give some tips on what kind of format it should follow or show us what your bid sheet looks like.

Does anyone else have a bid sheet for commercial bids that they can post so I can see what they are supposed to look like? I want to know if their is a proper format to follow.
I want to start giving bids on small commercial properties.

Thanks."

Brandon: "I have a good example."

Thanks to Brandon for sharing with us his proposal bid form. If you would like to download a free copy of this file, visit the Gopher Lawn Care Business Forum and either click on the free contract section or visit this link here.

http://www.gophergraphics.com/forum/cgi-bin/ikonboard.cgi?act=ST;f=9;t=5987

Search Engine Optimization Techniques.

This is a topic that appears quite often and is very important. Proper usage of search engine optimization techniques allow you to improve your website's ranking in a search engine. The better your ranking, the better your chances are of being clicked on when a potential customer looks up lawn care services in your area.

Our friend Matt started off this discussion as he was looking for advice on what domain name he should purchase or if he should purchase multiple domain names.

Matt: "I am trying to to think of a domain name, cause I might get a website going soon.

So a friend of mine was asking me, so what city do u live in? He said ok check and see if (yourcity)lawncare.com is available."

Steve: "My take is go for it! People will search out a city name way before they search out a specific lawn care provider.

This will bring you a lot more business."

Rob: "I would have a few domains that can be redirected to your website. Use the county and nearby cities in your domain names and redirect them to your main site. That way you are at the top of the list when a search is done for lawn care in your area."

Rodman: "First off let tell you this much. I am not be a master in "Naming Domains" BUT I know I am way ahead of the guy in second place. Your town name is (fill in the blank) then yourtownlawncare.com is a GREAT domain name for your website. Now godaddy names are cheap enough, I would reverse that name also. Also I would buy the .net .com and .info on both of those names. That keeps the next guy from jumping in there getting your google spot. Trust me when I say this, It's VERY important when you build this website, under the section "Title" I would just put your town lawn care also the county you live in and state name."

Matt: "How much has your business picked up from not (having a website) to (having a website). The guy that is going to build the site told me about Bravenet hosting, he also mentioned that he was going to build it for free."

Rodman: "I get 2 to 5 calls a week in the growing season. I still get calls from people from another county that I used to live in for lawn care. The reason is that I was first, at the TOP of the search results. In that county some of those pages are still cached with googles servers. I got 3 calls this week."

Patrick: "I asked this in a different thread before but I don't think you saw it...

Is it better to get all your keywords done in the HTML BEFORE you submit to Google?"

Rodman: "Yes get all your ducks in a row before you submit it."

Ozzy: "Hi guys. (ozzy's wife here) I think this is an area where I can add little input seeing as I am implementing an SEO strategy at work for our national company. Domain names do not play much a role in search results but I think the names make a lot sense for you since your company name is taken. The key will be your content and meta data. Google uses an algorithm that ranks your pages based on the content and keywords in site. Google also tries to be a little smart in trying to identify the area that your are in and the search results could be different when searching in one city than they are another. I suggest you use the city names a long with 'lawn care' in your meta data for better geographic targeted traffic and double use of the 'lawn care' keyword. You probably don't need to try to be #1 throughout the www but you want to be in your own city. Linking popularity from other sites also gives you an advantage. See if you can link from the top ranking sites. Some will do an exchange, but they have to be relevant links. You could lose points with the search engines if you are found using a link farm. Well, I could go on, but I will just a few recommendations to help get ranked in google's natural search results, although it sounds like Rodman is on the ball with this.

For every page on your site (with exception of maybe your contact page) **Your Title should not exceed 80 characters** but should include your keywords

Your keywords must be relevant to the page with an average of 5. You should probably **concentrate on two or three** because you have to mention these keywords in your content at least 10 times for a keyword density of 8% which should be the minimum. The content has to sound right though or the spider may see it as keyword stuffing.

Your description should include your keywords and and be about 150 characters.

Your content should be a minimum of 200 words and as mentioned above use your keywords at least 10 times. (this includes the use of them in your meta data keywords, description and title). Content is sometimes the hardest part for people to write copy for the search engine as well as for your audience.

Be sure to also use keywords in your alt tags on your images in your code particularly when they are links. Links should also be descriptive with your keyword as well.

I also happen to love google analytics. It tracks the visitors to your site and where they came from whether it was in the natural search results or a link from another site, the bounce rate, your popular pages, etc."

What great content! If you want to read more about this or join in on this discussion, visit the Gopher Lawn Care Business Forum here.

http://www.gophergraphics.com/forum/cgi-bin/ikonboard.cgi?
act=ST;f=6;t=6022

Why you shouldn't bid on huge jobs that are outside your scope.

At times we all dream of a big job coming our way that will allow us to scale up to a much larger level than where we are at now. But there are many factors to consider before you take such a jump. In this post, our friend Teresa finds herself in such a situation.

Teresa: "OK guys I need some help. I have been asked to bid this development. It is all rentals, they need mowing, weed eating,edging and blowing. This section is old military housing that was given back to the town then sold off. I have no idea what they are paying the people that do it now and apparently they are not doing their job right. The owner found me on craigslist "

Rodman: "Ok I will add my 2 cents!

I see a problem right off.

- One are you financially stable enough to buy about 7 more mowers
- Ready to hire about 10 to 12 more employs?
- Do you have the capital to operate for 30 to 60 days before you get paid? Some commercial accounts do not pay for 30 to 60 days.
- The size of this job is for very large company.

This is not a job for the average LCO. Do not take me wrong. If you have all the above, then go for it. That much of mowing will require all of your resources for the whole week. It will not leave much time for any other work. Do you know how much time it would take to just weed eat and edge all of that? In the grow season you will have to be there 7 days week just to keep it all up. The amount of money involved in this just to get started to mow it is huge. What if they decide to fire you after a few months? (most contracts have a clause they can OPT OUT) Then you are screwed with all this equipment and staff you will have."

Brandon: "I am not sure I would pass on this one. Opportunities like this don't come very often. Take a risk and go for it (or Gopher it!) You will never know if it is something that may make you a lot of money, or not. Say you pass, you will always wonder "what if I bid and got that huge job?" But if you go for it, then at least you could say "it worked out awesome" or "it didn't work out, but I tried". The richest people are rich because they took those risks! "

Teresa: "I am going over tomorrow and I am going to walk the place. Rodman I think you just may be right on this one."

Steve: "This is really an interesting point to discuss. Just to share my thoughts on it, I have seen many new businesses over expand too early and crash.

I prefer the slow and steady wins the race viewpoint. It's more stable. It allows you to make course corrections as you go.

You don't want one client you need to scale up for too fast because if they pull out, you could collapse. I don't think you should ever have one client that can make or break your business. It's better to spread the risk out to more clients than fewer.

You don't want to go into debt to buy equipment and have to rely on one client to pay it off. Because if they pull out, you will still need to pay this equipment off.

I haven't seen Troy on the forum lately, but if he were here, he would tell you how he got into debt buying equipment that took him over 5 years to finally pay off. For work that never materialized."

Rodman: "Do you have any understanding what it would take to CUT this much? I mean any idea at all? She will have to go invest right off the bat at least $25,000 in equipment. Then have capital to hire full times employee for least 30 to 60 days. Depending on how the invoices are paid. You are just looking at a BIG place to mow and not looking at the financial aspect of this whole operation. What happens if these people don't pay or miss payments? Now she said they are looking for new a LCO because the other company was not doing their job well.

I always say there are 2 sides to every story. Maybe they are not paying. Who knows? I'm sure every client you have ever had always paid you on time."

Steve: "I don't want to come out as if I am promoting go for broke when I say 'Gopher it.'

I have had plenty of friends who shot for the moon on a single venture, went bankrupt and swore off business forever.

That doesn't do any of us any good.

Scaling up, building up infrastructure, step by step, is a better way. You can catch even Donald Trump at times saying 'don't bet the ranch.' He says that because he has had friends that bit off more than they can chew and couldn't make payments on something because they didn't have the infrastructure to handle it.

I want you all to be in business for a long long time. It is rough getting started the first few years but you can make it through that time with a lot of base hits. Step by step, build your business and scale it up. Allow yourself time to mess things up, to figure out what went wrong and survive that mess up, to live another day and to grow another day.

This thing we call business is a life time adventure, let's enjoy the journey."

Brandon: "Why are you guys so sure it will fail? Can you be a little more negative?
Think about this.
Lets say the account would pay $10,000 per month. You make an agreement with the owner to pay 3 months up front with the remaining 9 months to be held

by an escrow company to be released on a monthly basis for the remaining 9 months.

She gets the $30,000 up front to pay for the necessary equipment, some employees (30-60 employees is not necessary), etc. She is guaranteed to continue getting paid monthly for the next 9 months.

Agreements like this are not unusual in situations such as this. I think it can be done if you use your head, a lot of common sense, and some positive support."

Rodman: "$10,000 per month would not cover her expenses. Let's do some simple math. Is $10,000 just number you threw out,why would you say that? Just shot one out?

1. Let's say she needs 12 workers.
2. Now they get say 9 hr. x that by 8 hours a day.
3. That is $72.00 per day x that by 6 days week, that is $432 a week per person.
4. That doesn't include a crew leader getting paid more.
5. Now x that by the 12 employs comes to $5,184 dollars week.
6. Now x that by 4 weeks, $20,736 month.
7. Now you say why would she need 12 people? Did you see size that place? Just keep up that would be the minimum she need. NOW on top all those 12 people pay payroll taxes, workman's comp.

Oh BTW not to forget, All the headaches that come with a major project like this, Home owners bitching, didn't do this, did this wrong. Just will be one big pain in the ***."

Brandon: "That wasn't my point. The point is she can make sure the money is there by using an escrow service to hold the money. You said - "what if they don't pay, she'll go bankrupt." There are ways to avoid that.

Of course she would have to take a close look at the properties to get a clear picture of the work needed and employees needed. No one, including myself can bid a job like this accurately using google earth. $10,000 was just a number."

Patrick: "I would have to say jump on it. If you can do the whole thing yourself and not leave out any other clients that you already have, that is. If you can see it in your power to do it and maintain your sanity, then by all means, GOPHER IT!

...of course, you may have to turn down a few new clients for a while, but I think it will be worth it in the long run. Build your capital from this job. Hire a couple of people to do the weed eating and the edging. Then get a few more blowers so you can all blow... then a few more mowers... a couple more weed eaters and edgers... hire a few more people... if this is going to be a year-round contract that you can keep from year to year, then you'll grow your business FAST!

After you've gotten the routine down pat, you can leave your new "crews" to do the job while you focus on the office work and some more new clients. Then, just repeat the process... hire a few more, buy a few more pieces of equipment. Before you know it (and I think within a couple of years) you could have 5-6 crews and be making more money than you ever thought possible.

STAY POSITIVE. If you can find a way, by all means, do it. Even if it means paying a sub-contractor for a few months to help until you can get some people hired.

ON THE OTHER HAND...

Steve is right, too.... this could be one of those contracts that you keep for a year, then they pull the plug. So be careful. I would say DEFINATELY sit down and talk with the "Project Manager" and see what their longterm goals are. Do they want to stay with one company, or will they go with the LOWBALLERS?

Be safe about it. Use your instincts, but don't just let this one go without giving it careful consideration."

Bill: "You have to go for something that big unless you plan on being just a small company. Take the risk. You need to make the jump to large company or someone else will."

Rodman: "Easy for you people to tell someone go out buy a bunch of equipment and go in debt. OVER one MAJOR account. That is not very good business sense. YES it's ok to expand once you have the capital and your business already doing well. It's ok to grow, I'm not saying not to. BUT look at the real picture. She has not been in business that many years. There are a lot of things that can happen with an account like that. There is reason WHY they want a new LCO, There always 2 SIDES to a story.

It just seems to much of a risk to me. NOT something a small company would want to try. Listen you have to crawl before you walk... "

Keith: "I've always been a big believer in controlled growth. However, I have to say that I'm with Brandon on this one.

I've not even begun to put pencil to paper on this as far as calculating an estimate. So, I won't even get into giving out random numbers.

When you bid jobs this big you do it completely differently than with residential jobs or medium sized contracts. You don't just give them a monthly rate then hope they pay.

First off, you are completely within your rights to demand credit checks and a DNB on the company. Have you ever bid jobs where you have to deposit a surety bond? I've had plenty of bids where I had to bring 25% of the first year's expected receipts in the form of a cashier's check to the bid opening. If I had quit the contract they would have kept the surety bond. It takes guts to bid contracts like that but that's where the serious money is.

You can make your own rules before you bid. Ask THEM (similar to Brandon's advice) to post a surety bond into an escrow account. IF the company goes bankrupt, you have a buffer of money due you. BUT, they won't go bankrupt because you are going to do hard credit checks before you bid.

Yes, they might try to opt-out half way through the contract. You are within your rights to make sure they MUST have a good reason to fire you. Have it written into the contract that they can only fire you for non performance related items. And, before they fire you, they have to give you three written warnings. What if they try to fire you anyway? Write a maintenance lien warning into the contract to make sure there's no messing around on their part.

Have the contract completely spelled out. Cover as many areas as you can:

- How often to mow.
- How high must the grass be cut to.
- How high can the grass grow before they must call you back. (if there is rain, you don't want to show up and be expected to cut 10" tall grass)
- Edging instructions

- Trimming instructions
- Blowing instructions
- Chemical application instructions
- Shrub trimming instructions
- Mulching instructions
- Insurance requirements
- What are terms of the supervisor signing off on the work
- ETC.

Get everything spelled out, leave nothing to chance.

Ask for a multi-year contract. This will help spread your equipment costs over a longer period of time and allow you to not be left high and dry after only one year. If you get the contract, quickly attempt to grow your business into your new capacity so you are not solely dependent upon this one customer. This is a real danger that Rodman has pointed out.

Yes, you might have to go into debt to purchase equipment. However, there might be equipment financing available that is tied into such a large contract. For example, if the job falls through, the finance company will take the equipment back. I'm not an expert in this area but I have heard of financing deals such as this. You'll pay a higher interest rate but it might be worth the extra cost if it helps you sleep at night.

Once you get all the above worked out, work on your bid. Bid it for what YOU must have to do the job. **DO NOT** bid it on what the previous company is doing it for. **DO NOT** bid it on what you think your competitors will bid. Bid it strictly on what it will take for your company to complete the work and make your necessary profit.

For a job this big, you will be better off hiring employees and managing the work yourself. You will have your hands full fixing broken weed eaters, dealing with property management, and dealing with resident concerns.

When you hand in your bid, don't look back or second guess yourself. If your nearest competitor is $20,000 below you...so be it. You don't want the job at his price. If your nearest competitor is $20,000 higher, don't sweat it.

I definitely agree that jobs this large are chock full of inherent risks but life is full of risks, too.

All this is just my opinion so cover all your basis and bid it right.

Good luck with this."

Teresa: "Look, I did a lot of thinking last night and today. As well as I went in the rain and walked around. There are ALOT of houses in there and ALOT of people to try and make happy. I spoke with the property manager today as well and asked if she ever thought of splitting it between several small lawn care companies to try and stay local with the little guys? She said no. One person has always done it but they have always had complaints. I suggested splitting it into the three areas I did and she loved it. I get my choice of section. In looking at them I think the picture posted I have marked as "part3" will be the one I want. Now everyone settle down and help me with a bid. I usually get $40 for a duplex on a half acre. Just multiply it out??? Give them a break??? BTW this company pays a month in advance."

Ultimately this bid never happened and Teresa folded up her lawn care business for a job with a steady paycheck.

If you would like to join in on this post you can join the discussion at the Gopher Lawn Care Business Forum.

http://www.gophergraphics.com/forum/cgi-bin/ikonboard.cgi?
act=ST;f=35;t=6036

How to market lawn service to home sellers.

When people are putting their house up on the market for sale, they need to get their property looking top-notch. Lawn care, landscaping, pressure washing and a whole bunch of other services are needed. But how do you reach out to these people?

Patrick started up this discussion by asking the following question.

Patrick: "I was talking with a friend who is a real estate agent. She said that they have "vendor days" where all the agents in the office get together with local vendors and it's kind of like a "fair" of sorts. You get to put up a table with your information and such, and the agents go around collecting business cards, flyers, brochures and information from the different vendors. She said that they have landscapers, pressure washers, stagers, and tons of other types of vendors on hand on these days. She said she would give me a call when they were going to do it again. She works out of two offices. One has about 50 people in it... the other has 80. So I should be making some HEFTY contacts. I would recommend you guys to do the same.... call your real estate agents. Ask them do they have a "vendor day" or something of the like.

That also got me to thinking about this..... if they can have "vendor days", why couldn't we invite THEM to something to promote ourselves. I don't know that it would work, or what we could even do.... but I know you have to be able to figure something out.

Ideas? Thoughts? Comments?"

Steve: "You absolutely could.

How about this. Get an area, have it open to members of the public as a garage sale and then have spots in it for local business owners as well. Maybe do it at a local church or local school parking lot? Or maybe at a store parking lot if you know the owner. It seems like garage sales really attract residents.

You could call it (Your lawn Care Business) Mega Spring Yard Sale! You could sell table spots for $20 or $25 and this is something you could do in the spring and fall!

Another thing you could do is to manage the event and possibly do it at a church. Give all the money raised, to the church but in return for you managing it, you would be allowed to advertise your business."

Clean Lawn: "I asked a couple of real estate agents if they would be interested in purchasing 3 month contracts for new homeowners when a sale occurred with one of their houses (for the new homeowner purchasing the home). Most didn't want to spend any of their commission on this but I thought it was a great idea and I even offered it if they would be interested in using it for more than 10 homes per 3-6 month period that I would discount the amount for them just to help put my companies name out there to these new homeowners. Still no bites, what does everyone think about this idea? Should I keep pushing it to different agents?"

Patrick: "I don't know... I mean, it never hurts to ask... but most real estate agents I know are tight with their money. When I bought the house I'm in right now, it needed to be pressure washed REALLY bad... the seller didn't want to pay to have it washed, and at the time, I didn't have a pressure washer... the agent said "It's ok... I'll get it done for you..." I assumed he meant he would get someone to do it.... what he meant was HE would do it.... and he did...

Tight... very tight with his money.... mows the lawns on all his vacant properties... pressure washes all the dirty houses his name is on... the man's tight, I'm telling you... lol"

Steve: "Maybe if you have any real estate agents that are friends of yours you could ask them which offer would work best?

The way the real estate market is going though, these agents are going to need something to move houses.

It doesn't need to come out of their commission either, the seller could be the one that pays it.

Maybe you could market it to the home sellers! "

Clean Lawn: "That is another great suggestion. I wan hoping to get the agents to bite the bullet and eat the cost and like I said I was willing to adjust and make a really reasonable price for them to continually use us for homes they were selling but I did suggest it to a young man who is an agent and is starting his own lawn care business so my idea might be used yet lol. Thanks though that is another way I will push it too and yes, I know two agents and they are tight about money or doing anything. All they do is sell the homes and my husband has his realtor license but isn't active with it. They don't want to pay for anything but make it sound like they do more work than anyone else in the job market......I want to sit on my butt and just answer phones and.... wait I do that for my lawn care "

Steve: "I think the homeowners would be more willing to spend on something like this if it helped them get their home sold. The best part about it is there is no money up front.

You present the idea to the homeowner. You can say, "look the real estate market is taking a nose dive. If you are trying to sell your house and need something to help push a buyer into signing a contract, I am here to help you. I will provide a years worth of lawn care for this property once you sell it for $x. By giving the new buyer a years worth of lawn care for free you (the seller) are actually saving money because the buyer will think they are getting something a lot more valuable than what it really cost you to pay for this. So ultimately I will help you save money and sell your house.

Don't drop your house price by $10,000 when you can offer free lawn care for a year and it only costs you $x.

You don't have to pay me until you sell the house. Then I will start my lawn care servicing on the property. You can't lose on this deal.""

Here is a free flyer you can use to send out to homeowners trying to sell their property.

Looking to sell your house quickly?

Patrick: "Nice, Steve... but I would also add in there...

"During the first year someone moves into a new house, they are too busy unpacking, painting, tossing out things they no longer need and all the other chores that goes with moving into a new house. They'll need a dependable company to come out and help them care for the outside of their home while they take care of the inside!"

Maybe offer them a 1 year discount on THEIR new home's lawn maintenance if they purchase this plan...?"

Clean Lawn: "Gotcha and that is another great idea to go along with it. Thanks guys I think I am going to give that one another shot with it being marketed at the seller now."

If you would like to join in on this discussion further please visit the post at the Gopher Lawn Care Business Forum. The free flyer download can be downloaded from this post or from the free flyer section at the forum.

http://www.gophergraphics.com/forum/cgi-bin/ikonboard.cgi?
act=ST;f=8;t=5921

GopherHaul 17

# Overview of GopherHaul

Episode 17

Original Air Date: Nov. 19, 2007

In this episode we discussed.
- I added a new section to the forum called "**Help me bid this job**."
- Free flyer template to help you promote your own toy drive.
- Marketing gimmick. Should you cover your truck in artificial turf?
- Winter lawn care clean up idea and another free flyer.

GopherHaul hits a quarter of a million views!

We have reached another milestone in the view count of the GopherhHaul videos. Since our last episode, GopherHaul has broken the quarter of a million view mark.

New forum section, Help Me Bid This Job.

With so many questions on the Gopher Lawn Care Business Forum about how to bid a job, I decided it was time to create a new forum that dealt with this topic. In this section, lawn care business owners can now post jobs they are looking to bid on, along with satellite photos as well as what they think they will need to bid and have it reviewed by other forum members.

One of the first lawn care business owners to take advantage of this new forum section was able to win the bid thanks to the help of other forum members. Let's take a look at what he posted.

APLS: "Hey y'all I just joined up here because I'm lost on what to bid these jobs at. All the accounts we have now are residential but trying to get into commercial. I got an email from a guy yesterday who has some shopping centers he needs maintained. I went and looked at them and they are decent sizes here's what he wants

1st property: 550ft x 950 with 2 retention ponds and 60 palms and 30 smaller oaks and misc shrubs.

Included in lawn and tree care he wants:

- Pressure washing of sidewalks about 650ft x 8ft
- Empty garbage cans
- Irrigation maintenance
- Pick up any garbage we see on sidewalks
- Mulch beds sprayed

He wants us there 3 times a week to keep up on it

2nd property: is exactly the same but is 770ft x 550 wants same services as first.

3rd property: 630 x 610 and has tons of smaller oaks and about 15 palms and lots of shrubs. no retention pond but wants same services as other 2 places.

He might want a street sweeper but I don't have one how much do they charge?

He wants a 700ft x 8ft wall pressure cleaned what's that worth?

Also he has 2 retention ponds(100 x 75) he wants "cleaned" which meant we go in the water (nasty) and clean the garbage out.

If y'all could help me out here I have NO IDEA what to charge or what the price difference should be between having the parking lot swept or not.

Please help. He wants an answer tomorrow or Wednesday."

Brandon: "I have mucked out ponds before, and trust me it is easy to underestimate how long it takes. As far as the rest of it, try your best to figure how many hours it will take each one, and multiply it by $60 per hour. That should get you pretty close. Sometimes I will walk through my steps I will take on an average day at a job to get a better idea of the time it will take.

It's better to over bid then under bid. If you over bid, the property owner will most likely tell you, then you can compromise. It won't work to compromise UP if you end up underbidding.

Good Luck! "

Rodman: "Cleaning a retention is better to wait until it's dried up and bush hog it."

A.P.L.S.: "Problem with the retention pond is its not draining right and he wants them done asap. How do you charge for that?

Also what's the best way to bid a pressure washing job? He wants the back sound wall done(700 x 8) and the whole building which is about 675ft long and 100ft deep need help asap."

Rodman: "I would charge $750.00 for the pressure cleaning. Then the clean up, for both ponds, would be another $900.00 monthly. I would have to know how much you have to cut and how often."

A.P.L.S.: "Alright thanks man I really needed the help lol. Commercial is a whole new game for me, but now I will have a little better idea of it. How much would you charge this guy for lawn maintenance, maintaining anything under 8ft, and he wants the parking lot cleaned 3 times a week? This will suck because I don't have a sweeper so I'd just hire another company do do that. Does anyone know what street sweepers charge for a lot that size? "

Rodman: "As far as the parking lots cleaned, you will have to get in contact with a parking lot sweeping company. Also when you do make sure they have commercial INS to cover your butt. As far as the mowing, I would charge them $400 month. To be payed month in advance. That way you don't lose any money. There is reason why they don't have LCO doing it now.

Once you find out how much the sweeping is, I would say charge that all by itself. Don't combine the two services together."

A.P.L.S.: "Alright man thanks for the help. I think I was way over on the mow bid but I messed up and combined the sweeping with the mowing.

He wanted:

Monthly
- standard lawn service
- check irritation system

3x a week
- parking lot cleaned of trash
- sidewalks cleaned of trash
- trash emptied from outside bins
- anything under 8ft trimmed as needed
- mulch beds cleaned out as needed
- weeds picked or sprayed in mulch beds as needed
- clean irritation heads as needed

I bid a bit higher than $400 but also included parking lot cleanup and the fact I have to be there 3x a week to check it all.
My buddy says he will take a backpack blower to the parking lot 3x a week for a small fee lol. I told him it'd take a while."

Rodman: "How much was the total? With the clean up and monthly service?

I also hope you broke that bid up. Listed each job, like the pond clean ups on one bid. The pressure monthly service job on another.

Do not get mad when your friend comes and tells you he will not blow the parking lot anymore. That is very large area to be blowing with a backpack blower. I have thought might be good for you to buy one of those blowers that are on a cart. Have you seen them? Or if you own a tractor get a tractor sweeper! If you do not have one I know someone that can get you one at fair price. All those are reasonable things that you can do for the parking lot sweeping."

A.P.L.S.: "Yeah i have already looked at a few of those wheeled blowers I found an almost new lesco 8hp one for $400. I might get... I bid the the monthly maintenance with all that stuff I listed including parking lot cleaning (minus pressure and pond cleaning) for almost 2x what you said but I did it before I saw your post. So I don't know if that will happen."

Patrick: "My question is, how much time would you save using the wheeled blower in comparison to the backpack? I'm sure you would shave time off, but would you shave enough off to make it worth the purchase? "

Rodman: "I would say YES for a vast area like that. Any very large complex or parking lot. Have you seen the power those things have?"

A.P.L.S.: "Hey guys just a quick update. I got the job. We came to an agreement of $1600 a month and I also have the other parking lot for the same amount so $3200 a month for both.

I also got the pressure cleaning for $2000 for both buildings

And got the retention pond job it was ALOT easier than I thought just drain the little bit of water in them (1ft) and cut the vegetation in and around the ponds I got that for $900 and some other work he wants done so I'm pretty happy."

John: "I would sub some of the pressure washing and street sweeping etc. Do what you do best. You don't want to get every job get the ones that can make you money. As far as the retention pond forget it. How much is getting stuck buy a discarded needle worth? You fall or reach down and get stuck forget that. Sometimes you just need to say no."

A.P.L.S.: "Just got back on here.... I ended up taking all the work and I got it knocked out in a week and a half. The parking lots actually stays cleaner than I thought so 3 times a week I spend 30 min on it and its done.

Again I thank you all for your help, most of my residential accounts canceled or want a bi-weekly price so this commercial helps feed us till next year.

Only problem I have ran into is finding good workers. Everyone likes to try to find a way to screw ya over or half ass it. I can't trust anyone to do a good job so I have to babysit all the darn time and if I have to be there to watch them instead of doing another job why not just do it all myself? I've gone through like 8 guys in a week all who wanted something for nothing. Where do you find good people. And its not a money issue. I pay decent, better than a lot around here.

LOL now the guy wants some fence put up like 1000' of it. Good money but again I don't know what to charge on fence. It's 6ft chain link. Then after that he wants a bunch of tree work done($2-3k worth of it). So this guy will pay the bills till next year when all my advertising comes out."

Steve: "What should he bid on the fence installation?"

Rodman: "1000' - 6' x 9 galv chain link....................... @ 2.30 $2300.00
1000 - 1 5/8" SS15 sw. galv rail................... @ 0.99 $990.00
99   - 2 1/2" x 8.50' SS15 galv line posts.......... @ 11.48 $1136.52
495 - 2 1/2" alum tie wire......................... @ 0.05 $24.75
500 - 1 5/8" alum tie wire......................... @ 0.05 $25.00
99   - 2 1/2" x 1 5/8" alum loop cap................ @ 1.73 $171.27
2   - 6' galv tension bar.......................... @ 1.53 $3.06
10   - 2 1/2" galv tension band..................... @ 0.20 $2.00
2   - 2 1/2" galv brace band....................... @ 0.27 $0.54
12   - 5/16" x 1 1/4" galv bolt/nut................. @ 0.08 $0.96
2   - 1 5/8" galv p.s. rail end cup................ @ 0.73 $1.46
4.86 - yards concrete............................... @ 93.50 $454.38

       Retail: $5109.94
       Installation: $2336.97
       Total: $7446.90

Now that is if he needs to buy everything. Also that does not include any gates."

Wow! How about that for an education in the process of how to bid a commercial property. Not only did the discussion include how much you should bid but it also discusses if you should bid the job or not. Then, have you taken into consideration employees who won't follow through with doing the job once you win the bid.

There are a lot of points to consider when contemplating a commercial bid. I hope this discussion helps you. If you would like to read join in on the discussion further, visit the post at the Gopher Lawn Care Business Forum here.

http://www.gophergraphics.com/forum/cgi-bin/ikonboard.cgi?

act=ST;f=35;t=6004

Free flyer to promote your holiday toy drive.

Are you looking for a great way to promote your lawn care business this winter? Here is a flyer to promote your lawn care business toy drive for the holidays. Offering to run a toy drive really positions your business as one who cares about your community. It's a great way to show your community that you care as well as potentially gain some valuable media attention. Make sure you let the local media know you are running a toy drive to collect toys for children in need.

To download this flyer template, visit the Gopher Lawn Care Business Forum and click on the free flyer template section, or download the flyer here.

http://www.gophergraphics.com/forum/cgi-bin/ikonboard.cgi?
act=ST;f=1;t=942;st=80

Marketing gimmick. Should you cover your truck in artificial turf?

I saw a great picture the other day of a lawn care business vehicle covered in artificial turf. I just loved the concept because the vehicle really stood out.

Chestin from lawncaremarketingmagic.com had some insight to share on this topic.

Chestin: "It really is a great 'gimmick' to get people's attention, but I'd be really interested to know what they're doing to translate that attention into customers. Or at the very least, prospects.

It's great to get attention like this, but to be really effective you want that attention to translate into either customers or prospects on a list you can move through your sales funnel."

Steve: "If they were a lawn care marketing client of yours, could you explain to us what you would suggest they do to translate that?

I don't think I fully understand you here."

Chestin: "Basically, it's a great gimmick because it gets people to stop and notice. But what I want to know is, are they noticing and then contacting the company? Or are they simply saying, "heh honey, look at the cool grass covered car", then forgetting about it.

Yes, I'm sure they're getting some people that call because they remembered seeing the car, but to be a super effective 'gimmick' they should include something that motivates people to contact them immediately. Namely an offer and a call to action.

In other words, now that they have our attention, make us an offer such as '25% off first cut for mentioning our grass covered car'. Instead of the spray painted 'Lawn Care' on the back, include a sign that makes an offer and has a call to action. And make it an amazing offer you wouldn't normally make. Something they'd want to call about even if they already had a service provider.

At the very least, you should try to get them to visit your website to sign up for your 'e-newsletter'.

Again, the 2 things that are missing to make it super-effective are an offer and a call to action. "

Thanks Chestin for the very good points! So if you are considering this idea, make sure you have a call to action to get people to call you and sign up for service.

To read more about this post or join in on the discussion, visit the Gopher Lawn Care Business Forum here.

http://www.gophergraphics.com/forum/cgi-bin/ikonboard.cgi?act=ST;f=8;t=6149

Winter lawn care clean up idea and free flyer.

When winter time rolls around, a lot of lawn care businesses see their incomes drop and their customer ranks dwindle. Keith from http://www.startalawncarebusiness.com has some great ideas on how to make money all year round. Maybe you will consider some of these ideas and utilize them to keep your lawn care business humming all year long.

Keith: "I don't know if anyone else understands this but I live to be outside and this time of year gets me a bit down.

Clocks are set back an hour and days are shorter. It's cold and stores are already full of Christmas decorations.

I really do love this time of year but these first few days after the time change are difficult to get used to.

I've always maintained this to be a great time to reestablish your lawn care advertising campaigns.

If you are still running your leaf cleanup ads and they are producing customers, that is great. However, if new customers have dried up, now might be the time to tune your ads to a more generic nature.

I've always found that ads such as this work well:

Winter Lawn Cleanup
We do it all.
Free Estimates
(Phone Number)

The neat thing about an ad like this is that you can never guess what a new customer will have you do in winter time.

I have put up mailboxes, installed insulation, screwed in light bulbs, put up door knockers. There was even one wonderful elderly customer who paid me the same price as her lawn every week if I would do a quick weekly grocery shop for her. She hated getting out in the winter weather.

So, don't slow down on your advertising. Keep it going, make it generic, and be willing to accept whatever jobs are offered until spring arrives."

Steve: "Keith those are some great ideas!

I hope some of our forum members take this idea and run with it!

I do think the change in seasons has an effect on all of us. There is such a thing as seasonal depression.

Sometimes I wonder if it has to do with the day being shorter or just too many holidays at once. Both can be upsetting."

I put this flyer together based on Keith's suggestions. You can download it and edit in any way you want. It's created with openoffice.org which is a free program similar to Microsoft Word.

To download this free flyer, visit the Gopher Lawn Care Business Forum and visit this post or click on the free flyer template section.

http://www.gophergraphics.com/forum/cgi-bin/ikonboard.cgi?
act=ST;f=29;t=6144;

GopherHaul 18

Overview of GopherHaul

Episode 18

Original Air Date: Dec. 03, 2007

In this episode we discussed.
* Elements to include in your myspace marketing.
* Running a toy drive to help market your lawn care business.
* How to keep your customers from leaving.
* A great add on service. Cleaning gutters.

What elements should you include in your myspace marketing?

A great way we have found to market your lawn care business for free is by leveraging the power of social networking and using sites like myspace to reach out to people in your area. But what should you include in your myspace site?

I asked one of our friends on the forum, Tara, what elements she feels every lawn care business owner should include in their myspace site. She seemed to be gaining a lot of new customers from her lawn care business myspace site so I thought she would have great insight to share with us and she did.

Tara: "You asked me in another post what elements I thought should a LCO include on a myspace...

Some of the things I have added which I think are very important:

Contact info *make sure it is listed several times*

Pictures of us/employees if you have them *we don't except for my 19 year old son*

Any helpful industry links - For example Angieslist.com has been a very powerful marketing resource that has helped us gain several customers this year.

I have their link posted. If a person joins Angies List or is already a member they can read several great reviews written about our company from current happy customers.

Before and after pictures and pictures of properties you maintain or jobs that you have done.

I also put the following in blogs:

Fall Specials *you will recognize the flier I downloaded from your site =)*

Additional Service Offers:

Our Premium Lawn and Ornamental Service

Our Standard Lawn Service

About Us:

All of these except for the fall flier I already have posted on our website so all I had to do is copy and paste =)

Now the idea I have is this...

While my personal myspace only has people I know personally and a handful of other basset owners I have met online....I want my lawn and landscape company to have many friends. The more the better!

I figure that I get so many basset friend request with my personal myspace without even trying *so many that I have turned down some because I do not want that many on my personal myspace* that if I put a little effort into it I can do the same when it comes to folks that are in the green industry, or into gardening, landscaping, etc. etc.

I want to join some networking groups and put an add in the free classified area that myspace provides.

Anyways I am going to spend the winter months filling it up with friends. I want all kinds of comments about how nice our lawns look, what a good job we do, what good people we are etc. etc.

Then right about when we gear up to start the next season...*probably in January* I am going to start putting out a monthly lawn and landscaping tip bulletin. Then around March when we really start gearing up for the season I am going to do a search, on myspace, for folks in a 25 mile radius of us *I have already done one and there are over 3000* and I am going to go down the list and request a friend add from those people that look like they may be potential customers.

I figure I get an average of 3 bogus friendship request a day...come see my pictures that myspace won't let me post and you can be a millionaire or get a free ipod etc etc...so why can't I market my lawn and landscape myspace in the same fashion.

If I get just one customer from it then I have paid for the time I put into it...so what do I have to lose...right =)

Again I really do appreciate having your site as a resource. You guys have been so helpful to me over the years. I could never thank you enough!"

Steve: "I do thank you for all the great information! I am sure everyone else appreciates it too!

Do you have any suggestions on how you will build up your friends list for your lawn care business?"

Tara: "The first thing I have done to get friends is send out a bulletin to all 120 of my friends on my personal myspace letting them know that I created a myspace for our lawn company...

I have had our company myspace up all of 2 days and I have 15 friends already...all personal friends of mine

The next thing I have done is to add some groups. So far I have added:

Entrepreneurs and Business Owners Group

Gardening enthusiasts

And Cooperative Ventures

But ya'll their are literally thousands of groups you can join...

After that it is a matter of networking. Posting to threads, talking to folks, being helpful and offering advise.

I am a real people person. If you leave me standing for too long in the supermarket line I am starting up a conversation with the person behind me

Relationships come easy for me. In person or online...

I actually get so many friend request from my personal myspace that I turn down because I don't want that many friends on my personal myspace. All because I have such a sweet squishy basset houndie... "

Sarah: "I was just about to ask this question...so yay it's already here...

My only concern is spending time making my page look good and now there's a nice spam button when you request a friend. If I get spammed too much I could be deleted right??? Like if the people hit the button enough.

And before I was saying how I didn't want to post my picture as I didn't want a bunch of guys contacting me just because they find me attractive or whatever but since I won't be alone at jobs, maybe I could use my picture anyway??

What do u all think, good idea or bad??

I'm just looking for a way to add "friends"/customers and so far my tactics have only gotten me one...so any other ideas are welcome!!"

Steve: "One of our friends on here who was talking about this in the past was saying he tried to not add more than 40 friends a day in order to stay under the radar. Plus he was using some kind of auto friend adding software to add friends. So maybe that will give you some kind of range to shoot for.

I think you should use everything you can to help market yourself. I mean look at me I make the GopherHaul videos LOL

Yea I would totally use your image in your marketing. Why not take advantage of your looks! Maybe that will even help you attract a large friend list! I think you marketing you, will help your business stand out from others."

Sarah: "Yeah that's what I was thinking, initially I was a bit weary because of the amount of creepy people I attract on my personal page, but it might work, so far I haven't been working alone anyway. So I'll try it. I've got a couple photos of me in my own yard I'm putting up, but I'll get better ones this week and maybe you guys can do something with them!! That would be awesome!!"

Tara: "I am glad you brought up the subject of spamming. I too have thought about what would happen if I got a whole lot of people reporting me for spam would myspace shut down my page. I definitely don't want that to happen.

I mean how many times can you be reported as spam before they shut you down. Thats a question I don't know the answer to but maybe I will send a message over to Tom and see what he says??

Like I said I do get about 3 bogus friend invites a day. I always report spam but I don't know if my reporting it actually makes the myspace go away???

What I thought I would do is be careful about who I am sending friend request to...I thought I would do a search of folks within 25 miles of us and narrow the fields down to folks who are 25 or older and on myspace for networking *no folks who are looking for a relationships or dating*

I figure folks who are above the age of 25 and on myspace for networking would be less likely to report me as spam...especially if I don't start making friend request until next March when everyone has their lawn care on their minds.

I also understand why you may not want to use your picture for fear of a bunch of guys coming on to you...you are a very pretty girl BUT from one pretty girl to another I say in marketing, one must use what they have. That means your personality, knowledge, and by darn if your lucky enough to have them your looks.

It is you that has to be professional enough to be able to keep your business relationships that way.

A kind of example, my customer the other day said something like you little cutie you. Now I know these customers are nudist and they have invited me and my husband to a couple of their parties...

When this has happened we just smile and laugh it off...they know that me and my husband have been happily married for 20 years and that while we don't judge them for how they chose to live their lives we are not gonna go there.

Really what you have to learn is how to be a professional even if you are beautiful...and yes I would definitely use a picture of yourself but I would make it one of you working."

You can join in on the discussion at the following post in the GopherHaul Lawn Care Forum.

http://www.gophergraphics.com/forum/cgi-bin/ikonboard.cgi?
act=ST;f=8;t=6110

Running a toy drive to help market your lawn care business.

It's that time of year for the holidays and what better way to reach out to your community and show you care than by running a toy drive for needy children. You could also do something similar and run a food drive as well.

Steve: "Congratulations to Sarah for promoting her lawn care business by running a toy drive! She sent out a bulletin to me and all her contacts on myspace. In the bulletin she said:

We offer free estimates!

And we're doing our first annual toy drive this year for toys for tots.

Unwrapped, unopened gifts for needy children this holiday season!

Call for an estimate or a toy pickup."

Sarah: "Yes figured I'd try it! I'm going to try and make a short flyer for it soon."

Steve: "Are you going to be using any of our free flyers as a template or will you be creating your own from scratch?

Also, have you contacted your local media about this? "

Sarah: "I'll be making smaller flyers, probably half sheets, length wise. Still need to save money until I build up more of a customer base but I think this might help!

I haven't contacted local media...maybe next year!! lol! I'll think about it for this year, but I'm not sure yet!"

Steve: "I think what you are doing is great and it's a very human story. You are trying to help out. This is what makes for great articles. Don't feel you need to be more established to contact the media.

If you get in an article, it has a huge potential for bringing you more business."

Sarah: "Well I printed some flyers. I got 6 in envelopes ready to send out to some potential customers with a letter also introducing myself and company. I've got a few more that I'm going to go door to door with tomorrow around the lawns we already have.

I think it will work a lot better (be easier for me) going to talk to someone about a toy drive and throwing my company in there rather than just saying hi, I'm selling a service. lol!! Well you know that's what people hear...."they want money blah blah blah" and they just say no thanks.

I think this will really peak some interest...and I'll be thinking over calling the local paper for a start, lol!! I might do it, I'm tempted. Or emailing them rather. Send them a picture before then maybe a follow up with pictures of me dropping them off....hmmm

Might be crazy enough to work for two stories! I'll let ya know!!

Well so far my dad was the only one to give me feedback face to face. Him being a pretty big critic on advertising ideas actually really likes the idea.

I brought my flyer with me to work today and he started asking all kinds of questions about it. lol! This coming from a guy that will straight up tell you if it's dumb. So that's good news that it made him curious."

I hope this idea inspires you to give this marketing idea a try.

Join in on this discussion at the Gopher Lawn Care Business Forum here

http://www.gophergraphics.com/forum/cgi-bin/ikonboard.cgi?act=ST;f=8;t=6363

How to keep your customers from leaving.

One of our forum members was discussing how every time he seems to sign up a new customer, another customer seems to leave so his net gain is zero. Do you ever find this happening as well? What should a lawn care business owner do about this? How can you stop this customer churn?

Our friend Scott had some insight into this situation and I wanted to share with you, what he said.

Scott: "Take time to communicate with your customers. Don't always be a hurry to get to the next job, show the customer that you care, ask how there day is going, stuff like that. I have picked up a lot of other services with current customers just by talking to them, letting them know what other services that I can give them to make their life easier. For example I cut this elderly ladies grass every Tuesday and it so happens to be the night before her trash pickup, So when i am finished cutting I take her trash container to the curb for her. Every month when I send her bill by mail she adds a $25.00 tip for me."

Steve: "WOW! That is a great story! Did she initially ask you to do this or did you happen to know her trash day?"

Scott: "No she did not ask me to do it, I know she lives alone and I never see anybody else there when I am there So I took it upon myself to do it for her. After doing it for about 2 weeks she came to the door the next time I showed up to cut and asked me if I was taking her trash to the curb and I told her I was to help her out. She was very grateful."

Brandon: "I do the yard of this lady who is a little older and had a hip replaced recently. I do her yard on Monday and get there after the trash is collected, so I always bring her empty cans in for her. It only takes a minute of my time, but she really appreciates it."

Patrick: "It's the little things that build lasting relationships with your customers!"

I totally agree with this Patrick. It is the little things that make a big difference to customers. Such things can make the difference between keeping a customer and losing one.

If you would like to join this post, visit the Gopher Lawn Care Business Forum here.

http://www.gophergraphics.com/forum/cgi-bin/ikonboard.cgi?act=ST;f=4;t=6154

A great add on service. Cleaning gutters.

Our lawn care business forum members, Keith, owner of http://www.startalawncarebusiness.com, posted a great seasonal service tip. This tip is especially important for those in the Northern sections of the country.

Keith: "During rainy winter days it is important to keep gutters free of leaves. If gutters are clogged, rain will pool in the gutters. Then, at night when the temperature drops, the water will freeze and back up into the over hangs. This action will damage the overhang allowing more water to enter the woodwork. The wood will rot.

Once problems begin, repairs can be very expensive. It is important and beneficial for lawn care companies to warn their customers of this potentially damaging problem. A quick $100 gutter cleaning job can save the homeowner thousands of dollars down the road."

I think this is a great add on service you can sell to your customer base in the fall and spring time.

We also have created a free flyer for you to promote this service which you can download and edit. Visit the Gopher Lawn Care Business Forum and then click on the link to the free flyer and door hanger templates.

GopherHaul 19

Overview of GopherHaul
Episode 19

Original Air Date: Dec. 19, 2007

In this episode we discussed.
- Holiday lawn care business marketing ideas.
- New free lawn care business contract.
- Using ice melt buckets to promote your business.
- Buying poinsettia plants in bulk and selling them.
- How to send out commercial bid letters for the new year.

Holiday decoration marketing idea and contest.

Let's all get into the spirit of the holidays. I created this flyer you can edit and hand out in your area. The idea of this marketing concept is that you are going to position yourself as the go to lawn care business in your area. You are going to be the one that is leading this outdoor holiday decoration contest. If local residents don't have time to put up decorations, then you can do it for them and include some coupons at the bottom of the flyer to promote this.

Later go around your area and take pictures of homes with outdoor holiday decorations and put them on your website. Or put them on your myspace page. Then promote where these pictures will be and how local residents can visit your page to vote for their favorite house.

How can they vote? Either post something below the picture in your myspace site or send in an email.

Then you will choose a winner near Christmas time and possible hand out some gifts.

What kind of gifts? How about three trophies to the best decorated houses? Or ask around town and see if any other business owner would like to donate a prize to the winner.

Send out a press release to your local paper to let them know you are conducting this contest and how readers can submit their pictures to you by emailing you.

I also want to see the picture you take or are submitted to you. Maybe we can have a vote here on the forum for the best overall holiday decoration pictures.

To join this discussion and download the free flyer template, visit the Gopher Lawn Care Forum here.

http://www.gophergraphics.com/forum/cgi-bin/ikonboard.cgi?act=ST;f=8;t=6159

New free lawn care business contracts.

I want to send a big thanks out to our friend Tim. He shared with us three new lawn care business contracts you can download, edit and use.

- Lawn Care Maintenance Agreement.
- A Full Service Lawn Care Contract.
- A Snow Plow Contract.

To download these files, visit the free lawn care contract section at the Gopher Lawn Care Forum here.

http://www.gophergraphics.com/forum/cgi-bin/ikonboard.cgi?act=ST&f=1&t=877

Ice bucket lawn care business marketing idea.

Our friend Tony from http://www.amw-graphics.com wrote us with this great marketing idea for your lawn care business. He posted this picture of a salt bucket he created for a local lawn care business owner.

Tony: "Here is an example of some decals/stickers we made for a client we have. He wanted to give out buckets of ice melt to his customers but wanted his name and company information on them. We also made "Please keep covered" and "Use Gloves" stickers for the lids. You can re-use them every year too."

Steve: "Oh! Great idea!

How much should a lawn care operator charge for such items? That is fantastic!

Oh I see that they are complimentary!

You know that would be an amazing way to promote your business too! Can you imagine dropping those off to people in your neighborhood?

What would you suggest Tony? Use it as a promotional tool or sell it?"

Tony: "In this case he is giving them to his current clients. You could sell them, or give them out for marketing."

If you would like to join this discussion, visit the Gopher Lawn Care Forum post here

http://www.gophergraphics.com/forum/cgi-bin/ikonboard.cgi?
act=ST;f=33;t=6541

Selling poinsettias as a way to market your lawn care business.

Tim suggested buying poinsettia plants in bulk and handing them out to your current customers along with a holiday card. You could also give these out to potential clients you would like to provide snow plow or lawn care services to. Tim said he also sells the plants at a farmer's market booth. He purchases the flowers for $2 and resells them for $5. Great idea!

Tim: "Christmas Cards: how many people have sent out pre-printed Holiday Cards?

How may have sent out HAND WRITTEN Holiday Cards? I do hand written cards so it is more personal.

Does anyone like myself put a little something in those cards? Like a coupon or personal note offering any holiday discounts on winter time services or even a free cut & trim for the up coming season?

Does anyone send cookies, candy or fruit baskets to suppliers?

Just something I do when we send out cards they are hand delivered with a small poinsettia. This is our first year. Years before when I was operating another business we had over 2500 customer so this was not in any way feasible so we sent cards with 1 free month home alarm monitoring to all residential customers and cards alone to the larger business's.

Think about it, if you were the customer wouldn't you be surprised to receive a card with 1 free cut & trim coupon in it?"

Steve: "Great idea! What do you suggest spending on a small gift like the flowers for your customer? "

Tim: "We purchased #1 & # 3 pots total of 200 @ $2 each we sold the small #1 pots @ $5 each or 5 for $20, the larger pots #3 we sold straight $15 each.

I got these from the same place my landscape supplier got theirs from a plant/greenhouse supplier. but as you see we had to buy large quantities.

We are sold out of the small #1 and only have a handful of the #3 left so we did well with this.

We set up a both @ the Farmers Market. It is only open on the weekends 8-5 Sat and 8-3 on Sun, another way to get our name out there. "

Steve: "Oh that is fascinating! So you give them to your customers and you also sell them at a booth! What kind of marketing do you do at your booth?"

Tim: "We have business cards that we stick in the flower pot and whatever season it is we hand out flyers with discount coupons.

We did this in the fall (with mums) and winter with poinsettia's and flyers for each. Next year we are going to do the Spring (late Mar, April), Fall late Sept, Oct, & Winter (Week before Thanksgiving to about the 1st week or 2 of Dec). "

Tara: "We passed out mums for the first time this fall and have done hand written Christmas cards since we started 4 years ago...

Both go over really well...

Our customers think we are just so attentive and kind and we get a chance to communicate and touch base with everyone at least a couple of times during the holidays.

I delivered the mums to all of our customers personally during the first and second weeks of October. Inside each mum I placed a happy fall message that I designed and printed out on Avery business card paper."

Steve: "That is very interesting! Do you ever wonder if because you do all this, you have better customer retention than other lawn care operators? Do you ever ask around about that? "

Tim: "I think we do because the extra touch of giving something back and being personal with the customers brings them back. We have 100% return for next season."

You can join in on this discussion too and read more by visiting the Gopher Lawn Care Forum here.

http://www.gophergraphics.com/forum/cgi-bin/ikonboard.cgi?
act=ST;f=8;t=6488

Sample letter to get your business placed on a commercial properties bid list.

Thanks to Tim for sharing with us this letter he sends out at the end of the year to get placed on the commercial properties bid list.

YOUR COMPANY NAME

123 INDUSTRY DR
HOMETOWN, US 12345
YOUR PHONE #
YOUR EMAIL
YOUR WEBSITE ADDRESS

Mr. Customer
Logistic UAS
425 Royal Oak Dr.
Hometown, US 12345

Dear Mr. / Ms. Customer

Hello, please allow me to take a moment of your time. My name is ----------------- and I represent -----------------------------. Our philosophy is to perform to the needs and satisfaction of our customers. We do a wide range of lawn care landscape services and strive to do a professional job every time.

I would like to be considered for any and all lawn care landscaping contracts or jobs that you may have coming up this year. My company is professionally licensed and insured. We run all commercial equipment and do this work on a full time basis.

The reason for this letter is to let you know about the savings you can get from utilizing our service. We have been in the lawn care business for # years and we would like to add you to our growing clientele list. We are currently doing business with many businesses in the area and can provide you with a list of references upon request. Our service includes professional landscaping and design, seeding, weekly cutting and trimming and many other landscape and grounds management services along with snow management services. Our equipment is well maintained so as to insure you a timely service every time. We also offer a discount for new customers.

Please add me to your bidders list and please contact me for any sized job you may be considering. I am always happy to give free estimates.

In closing, I believe ------------------------------- can perform the job to your personal satisfaction. We are competitively priced with other services in the area. Please give me a call at your leisure to set up your free estimate and consultation. You can visit us at www.mylawnservice.com

Sincerely,
YOUR COMPANY NAME

Whom Ever
Operations Manager

We have many more free lawn care business letter templates. This one and others can be downloaded at the Gopher Lawn Care Forum

http://www.gophergraphics.com/forum/cgi-bin/ikonboard.cgi?
act=ST&f=1&t=1541

Or look at the top of the forum for the free letter section.

GopherHaul 20

Overview of GopherHaul

Episode 20

Original Air Date: Jan. 09, 2008

In this episode we discussed.
- A thank you letter sent to us from out friend Julian.
- Casey's website offers the service of removing Christmas trees after the holidays for $25.00.
- Rob asked about what profit margin he should shoot for and if his business' profit margin was his paycheck.
- With the Super-Bowl coming up, we are seeing more and more lawn care business owners jump on the buzz of the end of the football season with their own football themed marketing.
- It's a new year and many new entrepreneurs are starting their business. but how do you get funding?
- Our GopherHaul business book of the month is "Operators Are Standing By!" by Michael Planit.

An inspirational letter.

A new forum member, Julian, wrote a great inspirational letter I wanted to share with you. He wrote: "Hello, well after gardening & landscaping for myself & a few paying customers over the last 30 years, I decided if I ever wanted to be my own boss, I better try now before I get much older.

As crazy as it may sound, until I found this Gopher website, I never really gave it much thought to go full time. After reading many posts & looking over the many free template's available. I thought "hey I can do this."

So far I have just 2 customers who have signed a contract with me for the following season, more shall come.

Again, thanks Gopher for all the information your site provides! Julian"

Steve: Can you tell us a little about the mind process behind the decision of actually making the jump?

What were the sticking points in your head and then what made you over come them? What was it that was holding you back?

Julian: "Hello all, well really haven't "jumped" yet. I still work 45 hours a week as a purchasing agent. Just for now though. I have two kids so insurance for kids & I is one reason I must stay until I have a reliable source of income. I am sure every family person who reads this will understand, you must consider the kids with all that you do.

Funds were getting "real" tight last fall, so I advertised on Craig's list. Offering mowing & leaf removal. Upkeep of flowerbeds & prepare for winter.
Well I got a few good calls & many many NUTS!
It did get me to thinking though, this would be a great part time gig. Of course my idea died out fast when we got 3" of ice & then some snow came. That pretty much killed outdoor work around here.

Well about 4 weeks ago the owner of my full-time job calls & is pissed off. Says I ordered the wrong stuff. I said well I ordered what you asked for, he gets even more pissed. Proceeds to call me a Mother-F***** Of course that doesn't fly with me, I am pissed about it and have been ever since, but again, I have two very young kids, I not only need the funds, but the insurance.

So I come back & reread & reread posts & look over the many idea's lurking here. I tell my wife, well there are only a few things that I really can try w/o investing big bucks. SO here we are just about 4 weeks into my decision, to invest in my own business.

So far I have reserved a website domain and am getting biz cards & some flyers. I am also going to see about some graphics for the van & my utility trailer.

The previous folks I worked for were very happy & said they enjoyed having someone who actually knows the difference between a boxwood & a yew.
Two customers not only signed a contract (I downloaded from the Gopher site) but have PREPAID me to mow their lawns for the upcoming season.

So with the money I was paid, I bought a utility trailer. I have been landscaping & gardening for so long I already have many tools. My only upcoming investment will be a 32" or 36" walk behind."

Steve: "Now Julian, the magical mix in all of this which is going to make your business take off is your marketing.

Can you tell us a little what you will be doing to get your name out there for this season? How will you stand out?"

Julian: "I hope to stand out by teaching people to enjoy their landscaping & not let it be a chore. Set up the WOW factor for them. Everyone enjoys compliments. They especially like them when they are paying for them. Consider how many home owner's consider their LCO to be their lawn mower. I want to be known as their personal gardener.

Then you have to look at some workers attitude. Do you mow, blow & leave. Or do you look over the area, mow & blow & look over again to make sure it is what you would expect yourself. Not to mention, when you look over the area-there maybe more work that you can upsell and do during your next visit. Commodity sells cheap, specialty work brings in higher margin's."

I hope Julian's insight inspires you to consider starting your own lawn care business. If you would like to jump in and join this discussion, join the Gopher Lawn Care Business Forum here

http://www.gophergraphics.com/forum/cgi-bin/ikonboard.cgi?
act=ST;f=26;t=6848

Christmas Tree Removal Service?

Winter can be a tough time to run a lawn care business but not if you are creative. Our friend Casey was on the forum and pointed us to his website where he showed us a service he offers to his community. On his site he wrote

"Not sure what to do with that Christmas tree after the

holidays are over? Call us! We will remove and dispose of your Christmas tree for $25."

I wrote to Casey, "I absolutely loved this idea as soon as I saw it! I think you are a genius! Can you tell us a little about how you came up with this idea for Christmas tree disposal? Have you done it before or is this the first year? What will you be doing with the trees? Are you doing anything else to promote this service? "

Casey: "I just came up with it a couple weeks ago. Not sure why I thought of it, maybe because the season is slow and I have a lot of time on my hands. I realized that to most people, getting rid of the old tree is a pain and a lot of people are not sure what to do with them. I will take them to the city transfer station and run them through the chipper. Now, the homeowner could do this as well with their own tree, BUT, they would charge them around $10....not to mention the time and hassle of loading the tree and taking it down there....especially if you don't have a truck....it's just a pain.

So I thought, $25 is reasonable....I would pay it if I wasn't who I am. I also get a price break at the transfer station because I know some people. I am running an ad for it in a neighborhood newspaper and that's it. But this neighborhood is HUGE with something like 10,000 homes in it. That's all the advertising I am doing for it right now, but I will send flyers to my current customers. This is the first year I have done this, so I will have to see how it goes."

I think this is a great idea because it opens a dialog with a great group of potential customers. If you marketed this service, there is a good chance you will reach out and meet new customers. These customers will then be a new group you will develop a bond with and then potentially upsell them on lawn care.

We then ran with the idea and created a FREE flyer you can download and edit to use for your lawn care business. It's located in our free flyer section on the forum.

Here is what it looks like.

I hope you are able to use this.

Thanks Casey for the great idea!

If you would like to join this discussion at the Gopher Lawn Care Forum visit the forum here

http://www.gophergraphics.com/forum/cgi-bin/ikonboard.cgi?
act=ST&f=6&t=6655

Profit margins. What should you shoot for?

This section is from a post made by our friend Rob entitled "**What is your profit margin?**"

http://www.gophergraphics.com/forum/cgi-bin/ikonboard.cgi?
act=ST&f=17&t=6525

In the post he asks *"When you are just starting out we ask what should we be charging? And the only way to know how much to charge is to figure out what your costs are first.*
Then determine your profit margin from there. That should be right.

Well no one ever says what kind of profit they are making per hour after expenses. Shouldn't there be a general range we should all be in? Of course different parts of the country are going to be different but we should all be in the same range.
Do you agree?

Can some of you guys that have this down tell us what kind of profit margin newer LCOs should be shooting for.
I have found what works good for me for now.

Hopefully this makes sense."

Steve: "You know that is a very good point. We do often talk about shooting for a $60 per hour fee but the profit margin could vary dramatically depending on your expenses."

Tim: "I'm not sure if I understand your question 100%. Here are some accounting tips so you may find your PROFIT MARGINS.

Month-to-month these may vary. It depends on the cost of doing business, A/R (accounts receivable), A/P (accounts payable and/or Expense Accounts along with Purchase Accounts) these all factor into your P&L (Profit & Loss).

Another way is to take all your cutting clients, total all income from them, subtract your total cost for them (FUEL), this would be close. You can't use labor/time as a factor for this application. You can do this with each type of job/customer you may have, this will tell you how much you made profit and then find the profit % for each one. There is your profit margin for each service you provide.

Hope this helps or is what your looking for."

Casey: "I think he is talking about.....if you already know your costs of doing business.....what percentage do you add in to make your profit. How much percentage do YOU add to your total cost of a job to make YOUR profit? I know mine varies from job to job and person to person. I try to make as much as I can on each job. When you tell the person the cost....and they wince....that's what I look for!
Basically, do you add 15% to total cost for profit? More? Less? What is YOUR profit margin?"

Tim: "When doing profit %'s on large jobs such as hardscapes and landscapes you would have to figure what your geographic area can handle.

For ex. most landscape companies buy wholesale prices and use retails pricing for the estimate for plants total cost to customers and use a multiplier of 2 for the TOTAL COST of said job, this will in return give you approx 25-30% profit but after you figure your labor cost into it your profit margin would be realistically about 15% total profit. This is a common practice around here.

For hardscape jobs I do it a little different. I total the cost of all materials, labor and equipment rentals (basically all expenses) find the total add 15% for profit and 8% to that for overhead (my run time, permits, fees, office paperwork, etc).

Remember to do this PART, this is VERY IMPORTANT: *If you own your equipment, (mini-skidsteer, compactor, quick-cut saw etc.) you need to add the going rate from local rental company for each day that equipment is on the job to the bid."*

Patrick: "Well, it would seem to me that if you know your cost to do business, then you could figure out your "profit margin" by taking your cost of business per month, divide it by the number of jobs you do, then you'll have a rough estimate of how much you're paying to do a job... then just subtract that from what you're getting payed to do the job.

Right? ...or was I WAY off there...?"

Tim: "Yes Pat you are somewhat correct. The way you explained it would get you close. It would at the very least tell you if you should stay in business or not or at least tell you if you need to increase your pricing. As I have tried to explain a GOOD accounting system is crucial in any business, TRACK ALL expenses. this way you can actually see where you lost money and where you made money, whether you have a solid P & L or not. A solid business continues to be solid by making appropriate changes as needed and this begins with solid accounting reports."

Rob: "This is great info for people that aren't sure how to find what their profit is or needs to be.
But I wanted to see what you guy's average profit margin is.
If you don't mind sharing.

Actually this is probably not just a easy one number/word answer."

Tim: "15-20 % depends on the job"

Rob: "Is it the same as if maybe you were a journeyman in some trade or somewhere along those lines. Income wise? Or does it pass that? If it was about the same, what do you like about owning a business in this industry that keeps you in it instead of just going to work everyday for someone else and not have to worry about the problems that go along with running a business. And maybe making the same amount of income."

Casey: "You are thinking of the term "profit" as YOUR paycheck. This is not correct. ***PROFIT*** is the money left over after ***EVERYTHING*** has been paid....including payroll. Payroll (including your pay as well as employee pay) is an expense."

Tim: "This is 100% correct. Profit is what is left after you pay your self and all other expense. If you are only making enough money to cover your business expenses and what is left is your paycheck then the profit is 0%. Profit is what the company made. You must be able to separate the two, you never touch profit for personal uses, profit is what makes the company grow, if you are comfortable with this then it's all good and works for you cool, but if you want to grow you must leave some money for the company. Remember you have to pay taxes on what you earned personally from the business (owner draws) and what the business earned (profit).

When I stated my company makes about 15-20% profit after I checked it year-to-date it is higher. I pay myself monthly just as I was a bill because I am a bill to the company. You must be disciplined at this, seeing all this money you have earned and wanting to spend some, you can't do it personally. I am not saying you can't buy new or newer equipment with reimbursement from owner contributions to the company. If your company has no profit and say you only have one truck and the transmission goes out, cost $3k (I know from experience). Now what are you to do about keeping up with your customers and getting your truck back on the road? Profit should be a cushion, for hard times and unexpected happenings.

I know this was lengthy but I hope it brought some light to the topic, this is a GREAT ONE."

Steve: "Rob, Reflecting on this post now, was this more of a question on how much you should be paying yourself or how much profit you should be making per job?"

Rob: "Well I don't really know how much I should be paying myself. I take a withdraw or paycheck every month enough to cover the bills and other misc. expenses and leave the rest in my bus. acct. for things like if the truck breaks or whatever. Also for other business expenses. My accountant told me since I am a sole proprietorship business I don't have to do that but I like to keep the money separate.

I think everyone here is going to have different income levels because we are all at different stages in our business. When I think of how much I am making I have it stuck in my head as a hourly figure because before May of this year that's what I was working for. So I am always comparing my income to that. Just in my first year it's been more than I was making even as it has slowed down. We'll see as Jan. and Feb. go by.

Isn't a bonus of running your own business after it matures the income you can draw off of it. If it is successful?

I'm not sure if I answered the question or not."

Tim: "Rob one thing I see in this statement is what your accountant told you, now please believe me, this is coming from 20+ year of being a business owner with degrees in MIS (Management Information Systems), ACCOUNTING, SMALL BUSINESS MANAGEMENT. I am not saying I know more or I am better than anyone else I'm just backing up my statement with experience and education. BUT, "I would find a new accountant." It doesn't matter if you're a sole-proprietorship, INC or a LLC you should always keep business separated from personal. He/She is right you don't have to keep it separate, but it is best you do. I know this from fact, in 1993 I was audited by the IRS for a 103k discrepancy a customer did not issue the 1099 and I claimed the income on my taxes and in the books with out the 1099 and the customer reported the 1099 so RED FLAGS where popping up everywhere and in 1997, I was audited again for red flags. In 1998 I changed to a LLC, totally separated business from personal and I was never bothered again. These audits stated because a large jump in income (PROFIT) from one year to another and not separating business from personal. I congratulate you on wanting to keep it separate. This has been a good topic for me because it has hit home in how I learned a hard lesson from the school of hard knocks and the IRS. This audit thing is the whole reason for changing and keeping separated, if it isn't, then there is room for question, if this should ever occur. So stop the questions before they are asked when it comes to business owners and the IRS.

I know this is kinda off topic but I had to try and explain it in more detail about accounting and the importance of it. All of this will show you how you can get your "PROFIT MARGIN" easier by using good accounting and why you should."

Steve: "Tim, Do you have any suggestions as to **how much a newer lawn care operator should be paying themselves?**"

Tim: "Well the 1st thing I would have to ask is how many customers do they have are they full or part time at the business. 2nd how much have they figured for expenses, truck payment, fuel, etc. Total the expenses + the revenue = amount company made less purchases (your pay).

3rd figure your living expenses. All of them on a monthly basis. Add together all income (pay checks from other) subtract house hold expenses from house hold income and this will tell you how much you need to live on. If the amount needed to live on is less than the business amount earned your ahead of the game.

So from there the first year I wouldn't put any strain on the business or your home life, this is VERY hard to do getting started. So only take what is needed to cover home life bills if it is less. Set money aside when your able for the RAINY DAY, and believe you me there will be those days. You aren't alone in the feast and famine days. EVERYONE goes through them. Tough it out and be sure to stick to the savings schedule you make for your business and DO NOT TOUCH IT for any other reason than what it was created for.

Example: We have 5 different business accounts, NOT counting PAYROLL.

- 1 for rainy days

- 1 for equipment new & repairs

- 1 for business expenses

- 1 for the general fund

- and finally, 1 for petty cash.

Note: You can move money from the general fund to any account that might be short for monthly expenses. There may be a time that you think you have to but it can always be worked out where you don't. SO DONT TOUCH IT if it is there for a reason. This is called BUILDING a Business.

Now to answer your question Steve, don't take more than is required to cover household expenses the first year or 2 then you can re-evaluate your business earnings and adjust how much money you pay yourself."

Steve: "I guess another big part of this discussion is about keeping your expenses low.

How big of a deal do you find this to be?

How important is keeping your expenses low vs showing off to everyone that you seem to be going great guns?"

Rob: "I think when you are a new business owner all expenses need to be kept low as possible. I don't pay on any of my equipment. I don't have all brand new stuff but I don't need all brand new expensive stuff yet.

I used to get embarrassed in my little s-10 but I could care less now. It does the job and brings in good money. I'll buy a new truck in a couple months with cash. Nothing fancy, just what I need."

Tim: "That is the hardest part of the whole thing Steve, keeping your expenses low. When you are just starting out, there is a lot of upfront cost that you will never recover. So the first year or two you may not show much of a profit but you made it through the tough times so this is a big deal to everyone just starting. If the average man/woman goes out and starts a company he/she is doing it on a shoe string budget. So keep cell phone bills down to minimum and schedule your jobs in low mileage routes even if you have to move a mowing day on someone.

And yes there is always going to be the "Nickle Millionaire" at any business and they never last. If they do, it's a bigger surprise to them than to anyone else. EVERYONE goes through the feast and famine thing. I did, I have and I know what it is like to have little to no money to even go to the grocery and buy food. But determination has paid off for me. I sold my security business and retired to this. I really wish I would have done this type of work 20 years ago."

Steve: "Very interesting insight!

It seems to me, it's the expenses that is the bigger trap more so than anything else.

It seems we all want to look good, not just entrepreneurs but everyone in society. We all want to project the image that we are on the top of our game.

Rob you brought up a very interesting point that I wanted to explore more.

Quote
I used to get embarrassed in my little s-10 but I could care less now. It does

the job and brings in good money. I'll buy a new truck in a couple months cash. Nothing fancy just what I need.

Can you explain this a little more because I bet a lot of people reading this can relate to you. Why were you embarrassed by your truck? Who did you feel embarrassed by? Customers? Other lawn care operators or just everyone and anyone?"

Rob: "Well when I first started out I didn't really have any money. I bought it from my neighbor for $250 and put a new transmission in it myself for another $250 just to get started. I felt kind of embarrassed by customers when I showed up to do work because I wasn't in any type of company looking truck. And also when I was driving around from job to job passing other lcos in a little s-10. One time there were 4 guys (lcos) in a nice brand new Chevy and we were at a stop light. I looked over and the 2 in the back (same age as me) were looking at my truck and laughing. But this is after months of being in business so I didn't really care. Because what it took them a month to make working for that other lco I made in a week easily. Of course that's during the busy time of the year.

Anyways I learned that people want to see quality work. They don't really care what your driving. But I think it might show that you have been in business longer or are more professional with at least an okay looking truck. I think it also gives off a better image to your customers. When you can upgrade then it doesn't look like they might not ever see you again. Maybe kinda shady."

Steve: "Rob I applaud you for sharing this insight with all of us.

I want to point a few things out to you.

> **Quote**
> One time their was 4 guys (lcos) in a nice brand new chevy and we were at a stop light. I looked over and the 2 in the back (same age as me) were looking at my truck and laughing.

As far as this specific situation goes. The 2 guys in the back were laughing? I am guessing that they were sitting in the back because they weren't owners. They were laughing because you are a shinning example right in their face that you are in the drivers seat and you are making it happen without having to go into debt to buy a brand new truck. They use all these excuses to allow themselves to stay as employees and they fear venturing off to do what you are doing now. They laugh because it makes them uncomfortable that you called them out on their excuses. It's nervous laughter. Let them laugh. You are a success in my book."

Using football games in your lawn care business marketing.

There are always a lot of creative ideas flowing around on the Gopher Forum. Matt brought up a great idea. Why not take advantage of all special events and holidays by creating a marketing campaign to capitalize on them? Here is Matt's SuperBowl Marketing bulletin (http://www.gophergraphics.com/forum/cgi-bin/ikonboard.cgi?act=ST;f=8;t=6834)

from myspace. Remember you can download this door hanger for **free from our lawn care marketing collection template.**

I like the idea!

What are you doing to promote your business with the Super-Bowl coming up?

Matt: "Even though the game isn't until the end of Jan or the beginning of Feb it's ALWAYS good to advertise a few weeks early, so that way there is a advertising window and you are getting ahead of other marketers. I will be posting the same bulletin probably 5 more times in the month. I have almost 300 friends on myspace now.

Subject: Lawn Specials 4 Super Bowl Sunday

Body: Having friends coming over 4 Super Bowl Sunday

Lawn a mess!!!!!!

Dont have the time?

Call J & M Lawncare / Landscaping

Would you rather be watching football or blowing leaves?

Yesterday I gained another yard thanks to the bulletin that you see, so obviously it's working. Leaves are still falling here and its almost time for the fall/winter clean-up. I see a lot of yards where leaves are just sitting there, getting padded down by other leaves,lol."

"Here is another bulletin posted on myspace..................

Fall / Winter Clean-Up (ACT NOW)

Weekends were made for living, not yard work!

Leaves keep falling / Choking your lawn / Lawn can't breathe!!!!!!!!!!!!!!!!!!

Overgrown Shrubs!!!!!!!!!!!!!!!!!!

Have you said the heck with the leaves. Let them pile up

Is your lawn sick, shrubs sad, down and out?

Our Lawn Care / Landscaping Company can help. We can clean your lawn up in one visit.

Have friends needing lawn service we offer a referral program. You have to be a customer in order to receive the referral program. No one time visits.

Give Us A Call Today. We Will Be Glad To Help"

Steve: "Matt you are doing great with this!"

Start Up Funding.

If you are just starting up your lawn care business and you are finding it difficult to raise funding to buy the equipment you need, you might want to check into this website that Andy used to raise funding for his business.

Our friend Andy got on the Gopher forum
(http://www.gophergraphics.com/forum/cgi-bin/ikonboard.cgi?
act=ST;f=1;t=6726;st=0;r=1;&#entry32042) and let us know he was using
http://www.prosper.com to get funding for his new lawn care business.

Andy: "Hi, I've applied for a loan on Prosper, and your endorsement will help
me get it funded. Giving an endorsement is free and will only take a minute.

You can help even more by bidding as little as $50 on my listing. If you sign up
as a lender and bid on my loan, you'll earn a $25 sign-up bonus.

Thanks,
Andy"

Steve: "Were you able to raise any money? What's your view of using this site
so far?"

Andy: "Yes, I was able to get my loan 100% funded:

I think this site is great when people need money or want to earn a higher rate
than a bank. I don't have good credit so my rate was a lot higher than I wanted,
but I always get a large tax refund, so I'll pay this loan off quick. If I had went to
a bank they would have laughed at me. But if you look at some of the listings,
you can see, people with good credit can get great rates, even for a car or for
whatever reason. The only thing I dis-like about this site is all loans are 3 year
term, so if you were to borrow 25k or something higher like that, you would
have very large payments.

You should all check it out, it might be worth something."

Steve: "WOW This is awesome! Ok so give us the low down, how do you pay
this back?

How does this compare to say, taking a cash advance from a credit card? What
the difference in the % rate?

Also who picked that interest rate? Did you? Or how does that work?"

Andy: "The interest rate was high, just based on my credit, and I could of made
it lower but I wanted to make sure I got the loan. Now what happens is I make
$56 a month payments to the prosper website and then they divide that up into
the persons accounts who bid and gave me the money, for 3 years, unless I pay it

off quicker which I'm sure I will.

I couldn't qualify for a credit card this high of a limit, so this was why I used this method. I'm sure as time passes and my credit gets built up again, I'll have a better chance next time should I need a little loan for something.

Now what happens that my loan is 100% funded and I have half a day left, is people want to get great returns on their money, so they start bidding down my interest rate that I'll have to pay, it started at 35% and its down to 30%, so when it ends, I hope to see that % drop even more."

Steve: "Did you have total control over what you set the interest rate too? Or was there some sort of credit check that this site ran on you to create a baseline interest rate?"

Andy: "Yes, they pulled my credit report, and my score was what determined my credit grade, this place is basically a lender like a bank, they also report my this loan on my credit report."

Steve: "Can you choose the length of time you want to repay the loan? Also is there any penalty for early payment?"

Andy: "All loans are fixed at 3 year terms, and yes, there is NO penalty for paying this off early, which is what I will definitely do because 25% is pretty high. But at this point, my loan was for $1250 and my payments are $50/month until I can just pay it off."

Steve: "Are these loans on this site just for businesses or are they for anything, cars or whatever you want?

Do you need to put up any collateral?

Also would you ever invest in others in the future? Or is it too risky?"

Andy: "No they have several categories, from business loans to personal and debt consolidation. No collateral is required, just your credit and verification of your information is true and legit, they actually will call my bank to verify I own my bank account and so forth.

And, yes I would invest later on, anytime you lend money there is some risk, but instead of giving 1 person lets say $500, I'd be more apt to give 10 people $50, you know, not put all your eggs in 1 basket. I think someone looking for a decent long term return on their money could do very, very well with this website vs. a traditional savings account or fluctuating stock market. I even see people on the website with AA credit borrow let's say $1,000 at 5% interest to then lend that money to borrowers at higher interest rates %, make sense?"

At the time of creating this GopherHaul Episode Guide, I checked the prosper.com website and found that Andy's interest rate had dropped to 25.93%.

If you are interested in getting involved with lending you can still take part, or if you need to raise money, try out the site and let us know how it works for you.

GopherHaul Book of the Month January '08.

Operators Are Standing By
by Michael Planit

We have all seen the different late-night $19.95 products on TV. From Ginzu knives to the Boogey Bass.

I know many of you love to create and invent things so here is a book that will help you understand the process of creating an idea to selling it on TV.

It's very fascinating and one day we just might see your product on TV!

Check out his business site here.

http://productstrategies.com/company/michael.html

GopherHaul 21

Overview of GopherHaul

Episode 21

Original Air Date: Jan. 27, 2008

In this episode we discussed.
- GopherHaul breaks the 500,000 view mark!
- Two 14 year old lawn care business owners will inspire you to start your business!
- A valentine's day marketing idea.
- How teaming up with a complimentary business can help you grow.
- Amy bought a business and lost a big client and now might lose her house. What should she do now?
- What should you include in your commercial lawn care bid?
- Who should you submit your commercial lawn care bid too?
- GopherHaul entrepreneur of the month.

GopherHaul breaks 500,000 views.

It's official we broke a half million views of our lawn care business show GopherHaul. The year 2008 should be a great year for the show as we reach out to many new viewers from all over the world! It's a very exciting time for us to see that others are as interested in learning about how businesses work as we are.

The young guns.

When you are having trouble envisioning yourself starting your own business and you just can't imagine it happening or you feel the odds are stacked against you, I want to share with you two stories that will inspire you to say yes you indeed can get your business started.

I was able to get a chance to meet two great entrepreneurs who run their own lawn care businesses. What's so unique about them? They are both 14 years old and don't even have a drivers license yet!

The first entrepreneur I want to talk about is Mitch. He wrote me a short time ago on the Gopher Lawn Care Business Forum here (http://www.gophergraphics.com/forum/cgi-bin/ikonboard.cgi?act=ST;f=26;t=6880), to say

"My name is Mitch, and I'm fourteen years old, and own my own company, I started when I was ten, mowing my neighbors yard and things have grown a lot since then!

I was very fortunate to have my parent's ZTR to allow me to mow my neighbor's three acre property. It's the ZTR I now own (bought it from them) and will run it until it dies.

I then made a HUGE mistake and got myself into a partnership with a good friend of mine. We mowed for two years, and on the third year we expanded into what we thought was a big business. Heres how the partnership went: imagine paying for 50% of all equipment, then getting bossed around, treated unfairly, and being treated like you were a slave. That was the business, not going into any more detail.

In 2006 I got wise and split the business, and being I did all of the bookwork, billing, and made all of the advertising, I knew I could make it on my own. I split the business in November of 2005, and started my new business in 2006. Spring 2006, I busted my butt and was able to gain ten accounts, which was just over my goal of 8. With my dad at the wheel, I was making a lot of money, and saving a lot of it too. I bought a ton of new equipment in 2006, all in which has paid for itself. By the end of 2006, I had fourteen weekly lawn accounts ranging from 4k sq ft to six acres. July of 2006, I bought the Toro Z Master from my folks. Just last year I hit double digit thousands, which was a lot more than I expected to make in my first year of a new business, with a parent driving me around.

I then started adding landscaping services, thanks to some projects last year where I learned A LOT!

2007 came and I started the year, knowing it would be a great one, better than 2006. By the middle of March, I was doing clean ups and had about 20 weekly lawn maintenance accounts lined up. I wasn't looking to expand much more. As of today, I service about 25-30 weekly accounts and do a good amount of light landscaping, hedge trimming, etc.

Either my dad or my grandma tows me around with my dad's Jeep and this year I can drive with my permit with my new truck! I just bought a 1999 Chevy 2500, extended cab/short bed, white, w/107k miles, flowmaster exhaust, and a lot of life left in it!

Right now, I plan on making this my career, and I plan on advancing into more serious landscaping/hardscaping once I get educated in that field a lot more."

Patrick: "WOW, Mitch!! Very impressive for a guy so young! There are other teens in the forum... Do you have any suggestions for the other teens out there as to the best way to run your business as a teen?

How do you manage through the school year? Do you cut back to the weekends, only, or do you service accounts after school, too?

What all kinds of landscaping projects have you/do you currently do?"

Mitch: "Thanks. As far as running the company at the early age, you have to act like an adult. I have yet to have a customer say "wow, you look like a fourteen year-old." The normal response is "you look pretty young, but by the way you talk I'm guessing your 18, 19?" And I politely have to say "No, I'm only 14." There is normally some jaw-dropping expressions. lol. Most mowing is done after school and I normally try not to work weekends, but that normally never works. I do my mowing Monday, Tuesday, and Thursday, take Friday night off, and do any landscaping that i wasn't able to put on my route during the week on Saturday."

Steve: *"Do you think marketing with your image in the marketing material would work for you or against you?*

When you are a teen in this business do customers find that a benefit or no?

What's your take?"

Mitch: "It would be a unique concept, but I don't think it would make a huge difference. Most of my work comes from "word of mouth" so people already know I am a young individual when they contact me.

I've never had someone say "I won't hire you because your a teen." Like I said, people know what they're getting when they contact me.

I do think that sometimes they expect the prices to be a little lower, but I display myself in a professional way, and explain to them exactly what they are getting, and that normally does it."

Steve: "When you reflect on your friends and those you know, what do you feel pushed you to start a business and your other friends didn't? What characteristics do you feel you have inside you that your peers just don't have? Why did you stand up and take on this challenge?"

Mitch: "When I was young, I started a small sign shop at my father's Pharmacy. I sold signs made on PowerPoint for $.50/each. I had a cash register, and a cardboard table set up in front of his store (inside) and I made about $30 in one summer! lol. But my dad sold the shop and we moved to the rural part of town, with five acres of wide open land (yeah, not all that fun to cut every week, lol)

But living in a rural area, I didn't really get to see my friends all of the time (out of school) so I needed to find other ways to occupy my time. So this did the trick!

Compared to others my age, I am very unique. I am motivated, driven, and a very hard worker. If I find something I like, I do it to the very best of my ability. I matured at an early age, which still allows me to get along with those my age, but also allows me to hold a consistent conversation with other businessmen, or older peers. For example, I don't go to the high school football games to pick up chicks. I go there to hang out with my friends, and also a few big business men in town have kids who play on the team, so I always go up introduce myself, give them a card, and try to get them to remember me when considering their landscape needs."

Steve: "This is fascinating! It seems a lot of people who find success in the business world had a support system around them of people who could help them grow. Having a family member who understands how to run a business is a great asset.

In a post not too long ago we were talking about John Morris who started Bass Pro Shops.

John, began his career in sporting goods with a fishing section in the back of a Brown Derby liquor store owned by his dad, located in Springfield, MO on the

road to Table Rock Lake and Branson, Missouri. That small fishing business sold homemade bait and worms, which proved popular enough that Bass Pro Shops incorporated in 1972. Read more here...
 (http://www.gophergraphics.com/forum/cgi-bin/ikonboard.cgi?act=ST;f=34;t=6361)

He started his business by selling things out of his dad's store too! So you see this is a move that many successful entrepreneurs have done before you. So congratulations on thinking of this!"

Then our friend Luke got on the Gopher Lawn Care Business Forum and introduced himself. Read more about this post here (http://www.gophergraphics.com/forum/cgi-bin/ikonboard.cgi?act=ST;f=26;t=6452)

Luke: "Hi I'm Luke and I run my own yard service. I'm only 14 but already in the lawn care business. I'm just getting started with Gopher but am looking forward to it!

Let me tell you how my business is going. In the mowing season, I have approx. 5 good,weekly customers. I don't own the most advanced equipment but it works. Just recently I purchased a new trailer and can't wait to use it this summer!

Anyway, right now, I'm having a rough time with the lawn care business. Winter is setting in but i have no jobs! What is the best way to get snow removal jobs? Also, I'm wanting to do some spring marketing with flyers, doorhangers, etc. Please let me know how to gain some new customers and "step up" the business. Any ideas will work! Thanks!"

Rob: "Welcome. Since you are limited on funds probably make up a flyer using ms publisher or something like it and advertise on craigslist for a cheap starter. When people call, be professional. Try to know what you are talking about since your young, and learn about what you don't know so you can be confident in yourself. People like to see someone who is confident and knowledgeable. I learn new stuff everyday that I am able to use when talking to customers. Maybe some of this will help you."

Tim: "Hi Luke, Glad to see a young man of your age working so hard and trying to advance. KUDOS to you.

When I was younger I would go to the neighbors around my area and knock on the door and ask to cut their yard or shovel the snow from their drive and walks. Maybe this is something you might try.

Or you can put your computer to work download some of the snow removal fliers from here on the Gopher forum and take them to Kinkos or Staples and have copies ran for as little as 0.03 cents a copy and start passing them out.

You never know one shovel job can lead into a spring clean up and then into a weekly cut.

Remember to be a kid along the way, that is important also."

Luke: "Thanks for all your suggestions and your time. I think I'm going to do use some marketing flyers for snow removal jobs. Hopefully, like you said, this will lead up to complete spring and summer mowing accounts. What do you think is the best place to place these flyers? Like, should I go door to door or just place them on public places? I already have a few on some local billboards and I try to hand as many business cards to everyone as I can. Also, I'm in a couple local yellowpages and phone directories which hopefully helps. I already have a few mowing jobs with my neighbors and local residential account but ts seems like the business almost stops in the winter. Thanks so much and I'll post some pics of my equipment and new trailer in the next couple of days. I hope I can keep getting helpful info from all you professionals! THANKS"

Steve: "The more people you meet the better. So letting your neighbors know you are in business will help you.

Another interesting thing that might help is creating a press release and sending it out to the local paper with your photo and talk about how you are a teenager and are running a successful lawn care business. That could get you a lot of attention as well."

Patrick: "I'll bet you could even get some of your friend's parents to hire you on to do their work for them!

Look at it like this.... every person you know that owns a house is a potential customer... every person you meet that owns a house is a potential customer... in fact, all of your FRIENDS' parents are potential customers. If you mention something about it to everyone you meet, SOMEONE will hire you... I'm very impressed that you've already had 5 regular customers! That is outstanding! ...but think about this, too... If they've already been paying you to do jobs for them, why not keep them through the winter, too... ask them about holiday decorations... gutter cleaning (if you aren't afraid of heights)... dog walking... snow shoveling... ANYTHING! Anything you can think of, talk to them about it... just tell them that you enjoyed providing them services through the warm season, and you'd like to keep them as regular customers... Then ask them do they have anything else that you can do for them... Don't sound too "desperate" for the money... Instead, make it seem more like you really want to help THEM out... When in essence, they're really helping to pad your pockets!"

Luke: "Thank you so much for the help! I really appreciate your advice and time."

Valentine's Day Lawn Care Marketing Idea.

If you run a lawn care or landscaping business, you are always looking for more ways to creatively market your services. Here is a suggestion from our friend Keith from startalawncarebusiness.com.

Keith: "If you haven't thought about it yet, Valentine's Day is coming up. I know the traditional gifts are Roses and Chocolates for girlfriends and wives. Lots of guys also buy presents for their Moms. Instead of buying $100 worth of flowers that will die within a week, tell your customers to pay you $100 for a flower bed "VALENTINE'S DAY - SPRUCE UP SPECIAL."

For $100 you can drop by their Mom's (certain girlfriends and wives love this too) house, blow leaves out of her flower beds, trim shrubs, pull weeds, and add a bag or two of fresh mulch.

As an added touch, hand her a Valentine's Day card saying the service is compliments of her son....and don't forget your business card. This is a great service to offer around Valentine's Day and Mother's Day."

We put together a Valentine's Day promotional free lawn care flyer you can download and edit and posted it in this discussion. One of our forum members has already taken it and edited it. Then he posted it on his myspace site and created a bulletin of it, which was sent out to all on his customer email list.

Another forum member, edited the flyer and said he was going to promote the offer on craigslist.com. I asked Rob if he will be promoting the special anywhere else.

Rob: "Just on craigslist. I can't think of any other way to promote it really. Any ideas?"

Keith: "Lots of guys buy their Valentine's day flowers from Grocery stores. I know lots of stores in my area have bulletin boards where they allow customers to pin flyers and business cards. I wonder how many people's attention you can attract.

If you put tear off tags with your company name, a red heart, and your phone number customers can rip them off and call you when they get home."

Rob: "I forgot about the bulletin boards at the grocery stores. Good idea! I'll put some up today."

Steve: "What about Valentine's day lawn care gift certificate cards that someone can purchase through your site and then you will mail it in a Valentine's day card along with a special message to the person the card is being bought for?

Maybe $50, $75 or $100 increments?

You know what else I was thinking that could be a really neat way to market your business for valentines day. Could you buy a bunch of cheap valentines day cards and red envelopes and then inside the card you could say. Why not give your sweetie something she would really appreciate this year. A clean yard and freshly planted flowers. Then have your contact information in it. What do you think of something like that?"

To take part in this discussion, visit the post at the Gopher Lawn Care Business Forum here. You can also download the free lawn care flyer template discussed in this section.

http://www.gophergraphics.com/forum/cgi-bin/ikonboard.cgi?act=ST;f=29;t=7057

Entrepreneurs team up with Co-Marketing

My friend Andy contacted me about his co-marketing idea he has implemented with his friend Jody.

Andy wrote: "This is a new thing we are going try. Mrs. Greenthumb is owned by a friend of mine, Jody, who just started up last year. She wants to just focus on landscape and design. Where I want to streamline and stay with lawn care & fertilization. So we double our advertising coverage, we are able to bring better service and use each others ideas in more of a tag team thing. We can cover more together than by ourselves. And our Trucks look cool together each our is own design."

Check out their truck pictures and join this discussion at our forum here. http://www.gophergraphics.com/forum/cgi-bin/ikonboard.cgi? act=ST;f=4;t=7027

What to do when your largest client leaves you?

Our new friend Amy got on the Gopher Lawn Care Business Forum and told us how she bought a landscaping business and lost a big client and now might lose her house.

Amy: "Hi everyone, I stumbled on this website just yesterday looking for something to help out my business. I bought a commercial lawn business a little over 2 years ago and it has been nothing but heartbreak ever since. I lost our biggest customer (about 40% of revenue) due to a state reg which required a re-bid every 3 years (the other co. underbid us by $100K/year!) and we've been going downhill ever since. I am desperate to hold onto this business since I am in debt up to my eyeballs. I'll lose my house if I don't since it was used as collateral for the SBA loan. Sounds bleak, huh? But I'm a fighter and won't give up. My big push right now is cold-calling, sending letters to commercial accounts, etc. Which do you think is more effective and does anyone have any tips on letters?

My advantage is that most commercial businesses in my area are not owned locally so the owner is no where to be seen. Plus I'm a woman (sorry to use the gender card, guys) but does that help or hurt. My husband runs the business with me and he has lots and lots of experience, but ultimately, the burden is on me to make it work (don't ask!). One final question, I'm thinking of changing the name to sort of get a "fresh start".

I never ran a business before but my husband was the one who actually started it back in the early 90s. Grew it into a pretty large business, then sold it to his partner. I bought it back from his old partner. I made a lot of rookie mistakes (trusting someone else to run and grow the business was the big one) but I'm learning! We do only commercial, which is a rough business. To make matters worse, the economy down here is pretty dismal so a lot of construction workers out of a job are pulling a mower behind their truck and cutting grass. That doesn't eat into our business too much, but that pushes the other residential guys into commercial. I'd like to stick with commercial since that is what we are geared for (big trucks, big mowers, etc)."

What should you include in a commercial lawn care bid?

Ok now this question really opened up a can of worms here because there is a lot of information to talk about so let's look into this topic deeper and find some thoughts on a solution.

Tim, A fellow forum member offered this suggestion on what to do when contacting a commercial property manager. He said "A brochure is a nice added touch to the professionalism of your presentation of your company. I leave a little more when visiting Commercial Accounts.

Not only do I leave a business card (that is a given) but I leave 3 cards. I put together a small portfolio, that almost looks like copies of my web pages including all the services we can and will provide (never assume anything, when you do you know what happens it makes an ###-out of-u and -me (ass-u-me). I build this in the MS Power Point highlighting key benefits of our services over and above the competing LCO's. I include only a couple of pictures of current clients and I also include a list of references. People make the mistake of listing "references upon request." The way I look at it is if it were I who was accepting bids or meeting with different companies for a service provider, and I had to ask about references when I have a company that has already provided them to me why would I request references from others if I have it in front of me, whether they were low bidders or not they would have a better or best chance of winning my business. It saves me time and "Shows Completion." The portfolio also includes copies of my business licenses for the area and insurance certificates. Now I have a COMPLETE package for their review.

You will find most businesses have to do things on certain standards, by this I mean before any work can begin all the proper paper work needs to be in order, If you go in there with the paper work already in order this is the advantage you will have over and above the others, keeping you one step ahead of the competition is right where you want to be.

The more professional you appear the larger your company will appear. With this paper work and such a presentation, the prospective client will forget how small you are. If all paper work is in order and they need you to start they may send you a letter of intent prior to sending out the signed contract and this is good to go."

Rob:

Quote
You will find most business have to do things on certain standards, by this I mean before any work can begin all the proper paper work needs to be in order, If you go in there with *the paper work* already in order this is the advantage you will have over and above the others, keeping you one step ahead of the competition is right where you want to be.

"What paper work are you talking about?"

Tim: "Hi Rob, here is a list of what I put into a commercial bid package.

Commercial lawn care bid packages should include:
1. Certificate of Insurance
2. Occupational License
3. Itemized list of work to be completed (Estimate)
4. Contract with detailed scope of work (include time schedules)
5. Additional or optional services (with pricing and time schedule)

6. Cover letter (thank you)

This may seem redundant and much but it is professional and clearly answers most questions a client may have, with out them having to take the time to call you to define such questions.

Benefits of this presentation:
1. Most lawn care operations only submit a cover letter and quote/estimate (This put you over and above or one step ahead.)
2. It shows clear detail you're prepared, confidant and ready to get started.
3. Cuts down on the "down time" having to travel back and forth getting this doc or that doc to the client, wasting valuable time for both parties. TIME IS MONEY!

Ask yourself these 2 questions:

1. Who would I want to do business with, someone who scribbles some mumbo jumbo down on the back of a business card or piece of notebook paper?

2. Someone who has taken the time to put together a professionally completed bid package with all required documents included.

I'll let my track record stand with the second choice. **95% + successful sales.**"

Who should you leave your commercial lawn care bid with?

Rob: "Tim, do you already have a bid ready when you are going out prospecting?

How do you know what services they want or don't want?

For example there is a store next to where I live and I know the owner. Just from going in there frequently and buying stuff. I want to talk to him to see if he would like me to bid on his property.

So I wouldn't be walking in with a bid already made out with optional services already listed, etc. Or would I?

What if you bid the hedges to be cut 4 times a year and he only wants them done twice a year?

Also where do you include information about your company? Or is this not necessary?

That's what I mean about the brochure.

If I go down there and talk to someone on a cold call in person. What kind of package or info do you think I should be leaving whoever I spoke with ."

Tim: "Glad you asked this question.

First **never leave it with anyone other than your contact**, always even on a cold call ask to speak with the person that can make the decision and answer or ask any and all questions.

As far as this store, you already have a rapport with this person so you can be a little more informal but still present yourself in the manor I know you will and that is 100% or more professional.

If this were me, I would create a quote letter. It is brief and to the point, no mumbo jumbo.

Then I also would attach an estimate work sheet (Which is available in the free lawn care contract section of the forum).

Remember: you're only giving an estimate on what services YOU feel should be provided to give 'CURB APPEAL' and by the way, I like the analogy it works very well as a selling phrase. You can always negotiate the number of times the service will occur, ex if you estimate hedge trimming 4 times and they only want twice spring and fall then you cut your price by half on that service. Only bid or show estimate for each service to be provided.

DO NOT show the monthly price.

You can give a monthly after they agree on what services and the # of times each service is to be preformed. You can break it down to 8 or 12 equal payments. You can make notes, if needed, on the estimate sheet and then make the adjustment when you write up the contract in the SCOPE OF WORK section.

BTW tuck a complete contract already prepared just as if they were to accept the estimate in full. This way if they agree to every thing, you leave there in one trip with signed contract, DEPOSIT CHECK, and signed estimate approval in hand. DONE DEAL.

NOTE: If it were me, I would create and estimate through Gopher Lawn Care Software. Itemize each service and frequencies of each service, attach to a quote letter, hand it to him with a cover binder and hand it to him directly. Include 3 biz cards and start negotiations right then and there at the end of the conversation. If he/she seem stuck on the edge one way or the other DONT FORGET TO ASK FOR THE SALE a lot of times when there is a hang up this will close the deal.

On this one you could add a little something about your company in the last page of your bid package, sometimes visuals are sellers.

Hope this made sense, just because it did in my head doesn't mean it did with others reading it, if not, reply and I will try to explain differently."

Steve: "What % of the time do you think a deal could be made on the spot like that?

Should a lawn care operator ever consider more of a soft sell where they present it to them and let the business owner get back to them? Or is it more important to say, this is what I think your property needs and here is my price, and then see if they will sign a contract with you then and there?"

Tim: "50-50 for me.

Hard sell or soft sell it's all in the feel for that customer. If you think you can get a contract then and there, go for it.

If you feel the customer will need time then give it to them. Don't even mention a contract to them. Give them a few days 4-5 and give them a return call if they haven't called you.

It is all in how comfortable you are and the customer is with you, whether you present a contract right then or you wait."

Now I after we got all that information out of the way, I want to jump back to more of the issues that Amy brought up.

I think the big thing in being successful at business is knowing people and reaching out to people. The more people that know you the better.

Here are some things to think about. Do you know people who work at these commercial facilities? If so, see if they can find out who is in charge of property maintenance. Are you networking with your friends and family? Are you looking around the area at local businesses and seeing which properties really could use better grounds management? Are you presenting them with bids to service their property?

I think being a woman owned business can help. It makes you unique and stand out. We have met many great lawn care business owners on the forum who are women. Have you ever thought about putting together a press release and see if a local newspaper can do a story about you being a woman business owner?

Amy also brought up the idea of changing her business name. I don't know if the name change would really do much, at least immediately. I would say it's time to hunker down and focus on getting new work.

Amy: "Thanks for the info. Actually, I do have a "portfolio" that is much like what you describe; insurance, references, etc. The funny thing is my references are great. The looks is professional, but we can't really seem to connect. I'm going the letter route for now and a got a ton of names from Sales Genie so...wish me luck. I really need it. I just dodged a bullet today by getting the bank to not foreclose on my house. Talk about having the noose tighten!

By the way, I just read the thread about what is included in the portfolio. Living in Florida, hurricane clean-up is important to know beforehand, so I include a price sheet of what we charge, man-hours, equipment used, etc. I also let people know that we serve on a first-sign, first-serve basis. In other words, whoever gives us the ok and a clean-up deposit first gets scheduled first. Usually within

48 hours. Just an idea for anyone living in an area prone to "environmental challenges"."

Tim: "Hi Amy,

Welcome to the Gopher forum.

First I'd like to say 40% is a big bite, I understand the panic. This is crunch time, tighten up the belt, pull those pants up, tuck that shirt in and lets dig into this.

Being a woman has no disadvantages or advantages in this Industry. I know a lot of women LCO owners.

You can crawl out of this. First thing is to contact your accountant and do a complete audit on your business. Look for every possible expense cut you can make, this is restructure time. **DO NOT**, I repeat **DO NOT** go out there looking for that one big job or contract to get you out of this, chances are greater you're not going to get it in a fast way. If you do get one, great, but most probably it's not going to happen. So let's get that out of your mind now. Look for quantity. The more reoccurring revenue you can generate the stronger your business will be. Do not limit yourself to only commercial jobs, get out there and hit up the residential market just as hard as if you where just getting started in business. Hit those residential areas multiple times, not just once. You have an advantage on the trunk slammers. You are established so use it to your advantage. Then slam those potential small business customers the same way, with letters and mailers, cold call, and phone calls. Get in their face. Step it up a notch. The accounting dept. or GM of the larger commercial facilities are the ones to contact most generally for being put on the bidders list.

Do you provide any of these services?

- Landscaping (new & renovation)
- Hardscapes (Patios, Driveway pavers, retaining wall or accent stone)
- Lawn, shrub, tree application programs

Do you have any architect's, home builders or general contractors that you work with? If not, you need to get started on a list to provide services to them.

Do you receive any new construction reports, such as The Dodge Reports, Bid Clerk, or Construction Manager subscriptions? If not get it.

You really need to use your many years of established business to your advantage. I would NOT change the name at this time unless there are REALLY good reasons to do so.

Use your network to the fullest. All your current customers are your network. Offer the management discounted rates to service their homes.

If you have SBA loan then you can ask for extensions and generally you will get them, providing the circumstances. The bank does not want your house. They will work with you even if every 3 months you make one interest payment. Don't let the media push the bad economy scare off on you. It is a political tactic and history has proven by the time the media realizes we are in a recession, it is almost over. This isn't a political issue this is about getting your company back up on its feet and running strong. So let's get at it hard and full throttle.

Use your friends and family network the same as if they where already customers. Join a BNI Group, it's a great network to get good referrals from, takes some work but it is worth it in the long run.

You might want to set some short term goals. Plan from those goals and push it. If you don't have outside sales get some and put them on a commission only pay. You will have to pay more for this type of sales person but it works out better for you. When they bring you a deposit check, you pay them. Done deal. Outside sales helps you by spreading your company name to more businesses and follow up on those letters you're going to send out. Three sales personnel will be able to hit 8-10 potential customers per day each. That is 30 per day times 5 days total of 150 businesses per week. Try it. If it didn't work, TruGreen would not be doing it every year all over the country. Time is getting short for you on the start of the new season so you don't have much time to get this in order. So work fast, stay focused, and GOOD LUCK!"

Steve: "Tim, I really think you are dead on with this. When you are in survival mode, you don't want to swing for the fences. You want a lot of quick base hits to help turn the tide and improve your chances of survival.

Once you can see things are picking up and you are landing more smaller clients, you are going to feel like you can breathe again.

We all tend to go into panic mode when disasters hit and it is at that time we tend to make the worst decisions. We tend to make a bad situation worse and we do that quickly."

Amy: "Thanks Tim and Steve, you are right about the smaller accounts. I have definitely gotten away from the mid-set that the 10K/mo account is the one I want. Basically, profit is the same and you don't have to sweat it if you lose it. Besides, those really big ones can be a real pain in the $&*#. The smaller ones don't act like you're at their mercy. I have had both and can say that the smaller ones are more loyal.

As far as cutting costs, we are running about as lean as we can right now. Our biggest expenses are fuel, payroll and the payment on the SBA (which is interest only right now). Other than that, we've pretty much cut everything out. My crew chief is great with engine repair so he is doing double duty as mechanic.

By they way, how do you get in with developers? I know they tend to use their own landscapers until the project is 90% built out. I'd love to get in on that. Nice fat budgets on those!

Can I ask a favor, though? Would you mind reading the letter I'm sending out and give me some tips on what you think. I'd really appreciate it. I'm enclosing a magnetized business card with it. Amy

Dear General Manager

Everything in our County seems to have come to a standstill. Even the grass seems to have stopped growing. But that shouldn't mean your landscape contractor has taken the winter off. The cooler temperatures provide an excellent time for fertilization and weed control, as well as getting those clogged sprinkler heads working. And when was the last time the owner of your landscape provider paid you a visit to check on the progress of your maintenance program? Just because the economy has come to a screeching halt shouldn't mean your service does as well.

*Our Lawn Care Company is a family-owned, commercial landscaping contractor which has provided unrivaled service to the Tri-County area for over 15 years. Because we only service commercial accounts, such as *****, we are especially sensitive and pro-active to the unique needs of a property of your size. You can speak to the owner of our business at any time, and be confident* *knowing that your needs will be addressed immediately. Besides, I can't let you down. My customers pay my mortgage and if they're not happy, I'd become just another dismal statistic.*

If you would like a complimentary landscape maintenance bid, please give me a call on my cell phone at 888-555-0001 . I look forward to meeting with you!

Sincerely, Amy"

Tim: "Your letter is nice but you never want to talk politics or religion to clients, nor do you want to say anything that my sound desperate.

Developers are a little tricky to get in with. By tricky I mean you really have to be in their face and once they have a service provider they like, it is tough to break up that marriage.

If you don't mind I have made some light edits to your letter and I wish you luck.

Your Lawn Care Company
Your Address Here
City, ST, ZIP
PHONE
DATE

Contact Name
Company Name.
Address.
City, ST ZIP

Dear Contact Name,

*Hello, please allow me to take a moment of your time. My name is Amy ------?
And I represent Your Lawn Care Company. Our philosophy is to perform to the needs and satisfaction of our customers. We do a wide range of property maintenance services and strive to do a professional job every time.*

I would like to be considered for any and all Property Maintenance contracts or jobs that you may have coming up this year. My company is professionally licensed and insured. We run all commercial equipment and do this work on a full time basis.

The reason for this letter is to let you know about the savings you can get from utilizing our service. Your Lawn Care Company is a family-owned, commercial landscaping contractor which has provided unrivaled service to the Tri-County area for over 15 years. We provide services for commercial accounts, such as *****, we are especially sensitive and pro-active to the unique needs of a property of your size. You can speak to me at any time, and be confident knowing that your needs will be addressed immediately. Our equipment is well maintained so as to insure you a timely service every time. We also offer a discount for new customers.

Please add me to your bidders list and please contact me for any size job you may be considering. I am always happy to give free estimates.

In closing, I believe Your Lawn Care Company can perform the job to your personal satisfaction. We are competitively priced with other services in the area. Please give me a call at your leisure to set up your free estimate and consultation. You can visit us at LIST YOUR WEBSITE.

Sincerely,
Your lawn Care Company

Amy
Owner "

Keith from startalawncarebusiness.com had this to say.

"I am jumping in on this thread a bit late.

Something in your initial post struck me a bit odd (forgive me if you've covered it and I overlooked it).

You lost a major lawn care contract when a company underbid you by $100K. Is that $100K over the life of the contract? or per year?

Tell us more about that contract.

If we can analyze what when wrong on this contract we can give you good direction for future projects.

What was your company's bid before you were underbid?
Do you think the other company will be able to do the work and not go broke? If this is the case, why did your company need to bid so high for the contract? $100K over is not a competitive bid on your part.

Is this contract congruent with the type of work your company regularly targets? If so, I imagine you have a hefty equipment list. Will that equipment translate into smaller jobs or do you need to downsize into more economical machinery?

What is your current equipment list and what type jobs are you already set up to do?

If you have a good deal of experience with large scale contracts and you have the equipment to manage this work, it might be better to beat the bushes and uncover other substantial contracts that will go well with your equipment and experience than to drastically change your M.O.

Since you are already recognized as a large-scale provider, I am sure you are on every bid list in town. You should be receiving bid requests weekly this time of year.

I definitely agree with Tim that you don't want to swing for the fences. But, 25 medium sized business and large residential lawn care jobs might be more in your line of work than 200 small residential jobs.

We had a thread going here on the Gopher forums a couple weeks ago about going after large contracts and the dangers of a company putting too many eggs in one basket. This sounds like a good case to learn from.

Thanks for letting me add my 2 cents."

WOW was this an absolutely incredible discussion. I want to make reference to a couple of Gopher Lawn Care Forum posts here so you can jump into the conversation and get involved more if you choose.

http://www.gophergraphics.com/forum/cgi-bin/ikonboard.cgi?
act=ST;f=26;t=7060;

and

http://www.gophergraphics.com/forum/cgi-bin/ikonboard.cgi?
act=ST;f=9;t=6968

Entrepreneur of the Month.

This episode of GopherHaul is in memory of Richard Knerr founder of Wham-o.
He and his boyhood best friend started the company in 1948. He brought the
hula hoop, the frisbee, hackie sack and many other great products to all of us.

To read more about Richard or join in on a discussion of him, visit the Gopher
Forum here.

http://www.gophergraphics.com/forum/cgi-bin/ikonboard.cgi?
act=ST;f=34;t=6987

GopherHaul 22

Overview of GopherHaul

Episode #22

Original Air Date: February 15, 2008

In this episode we discussed.
- GopherHaul breaks the 600,000 view mark!
- GopherHaul podcasts through Skype.com
- Inspirational letter from Jared.
- Fernando's election time marketing idea.
- Season prepay question.
- Neighborhood yard sale marketing idea.
- GopherHaul business book of the month.

GopherHaul breaks 600,000 views.

GOPHERHAUL REACHES 600,000 views! And GopherHaul has it's own page now on the Lawn And Garden Webvision website.

http://www.lawnandgardenwv.com

GopherHaul podcasts online.

We created a skype.com internet chat and phone account which is a free service and program you can download. Add user GopherHaul to you contact list and check out our forum for a future Gopher Lawn Care Forum discussion and podcast. You can review all previous podcasts on our Odeo podcast channel at
http://odeo.com/channel/797663/view
Also
http://www.talkshoe.com/tc/15950
or use your Apple iTunes and do a search for the GopherHaul podcasts.

New inspiration letter from Jared.

A new forum member and friend, Jared contacted the Gopher Lawn Care Forum in this post:
http://www.gophergraphics.com/forum/cgi-bin/ikonboard.cgi?act=ST;f=26;t=7090

Jared: "Hi, my name is Jared and this is the first time I've posted on the Gopher Forum. Last year I started a small lawn care business.

I've got to say this site is GREAT! I can't believe all of the information and sample documents. It's great to see so many people sharing resources, It's really commendable. I've tapped into many of them for advertisement ideas and customer letters.

My landscaping business was started as a side gig to compliment my full time teaching job, but it's quickly becoming a real passion of mine. I did a lot of hardscape work while I was in college, but I never did much mowing. After college from time to time I would help friends in the business with hardscape jobs and in the process I learned a thing or two about mowing.

After some time it go to the point where I was like "**I should start doing this work on my own**."

Now get out there and start your business! There is no reason why you can't. There is so much free information on the Gopher Forum you can get everything you need to get started! You can also check out our blog too at http://www.lawnchat.com

Fernando's election time marketing idea.

Fernando posted a very creative idea that just took off. You can visit the link on the Gopher Lawn Care Forum here http://www.gophergraphics.com/forum/cgi-bin/ikonboard.cgi?act=ST;f=8;t=7155

In this post Fernando wrote "I have an advertising idea! Since all we see in the news is the elections, why not make flyers about "chose/vote/elect the right Lawn Care Company" with true promising results - for your lawn care needs....,
lol, something like that.
Any ideas?"

Then I jumped in with some more creative marketing ideas by saying "what if you created a marketing campaign that looked like an election campaign and put up lawn signs all over the place?

Something like vote for Fernando of Your Lawn Care Business.

Something that would get people to scratch their heads and wonder if you are really running for something or if it was a commercial ad! That would be really hilarious and it just might work because then your ads might not get pulled down from street corners!

You could also create flyers that say something like Vote Fernando, "I promise a beautiful lush green lawn for all my constituents!"

Maybe make door hangers.

Then you could register and create a website that says something like voteforfernando.com and have a picture of you on the main page and what your 'campaign promises' are.

If you vote for me to service your lawn, I will promise the following ....

This could really create a buzz worthy marketing campaign for you.

Maybe people wouldn't know you were actually promoting your lawn care business until they went to your web site. Wouldn't that be a blast! So all over the place would be these signs that say vote for Fernando of the 'lawn party.'

LOL And then to find out more people would go to your votefernando.com site and find out you are running to be elected as their lawn care provider!

I bet you would get media attention for this marketing campaign

What an idea!

You could also make tshirts up that promote this as well and get all your friends to wear them."

Fernando and I had a chance one night to brainstorm about this idea more on a skype.com call and we came up with more ideas.

I suggested to him "I was thinking you could include some 'issues' your campaign is going to deal with on your website. Ideas for your 'campaign issues'?

Here are some I made up that are comical spins on real campaign issues:

- Everyone will have the Absolute Right To Ownership of a Beautiful Lawn
- You will not raise prices on lawn care
- You want to make sure everyone homeowner has access to affordable lawn care services.
- You will also make sure every customer is treated in a friendly manner.
- Homeland Security: You will assist in Homeland Security by keeping hedges around windows properly maintained.
- Education: You will help educate the customer by explaining to them the different services they may need to obtain their ideal lawn.
- Energy: You promise to use more energy efficient lawn care power equipment to cut back on global warming.
- Housing: You promise to offer your services to all the homes in your neighborhood.
- Economic stimulus: You will promise to buy your supplies from other local businesses.

Also make sure when you get your lawn signs you stick one at the entrance of the local paper's parking lot.

What if on your website, you didn't explain anything more about what you are doing until a certain date. You could say on the website, you will explain your platform on 3/15 so please check back in.

This could build up buzz and get people wondering what the heck you are doing. Then on 3/14 send out a press release to the paper explaining it was a marketing stunt to promote your lawn care business.

You could also create a video on your website, hosted on youtube, that welcomed them to your site and they should return on 3/15 when you will be announcing your candidacy run."

Maybe some of these ideas will inspire you to think creatively the next time you are trying to promote your lawn care business around the time of elections.

Season prepay question.

"Is it a good idea to offer a discount for a full season pre-payment or prepay?"

A new forum member and friend of ours Rebecca posted a great question on the forum. You can visit the post here and join in on the discussion if you'd like http://www.gophergraphics.com/forum/cgi-bin/ikonboard.cgi?act=ST;f=9;t=7229;

Rebecca: "Ok, I'll ask one more question then leave you guys alone. We have heard that a lot of companies in this area offer their customers a discount if they pay the entire season in full before the season starts. Is this a good idea? If so, do we offer it only to the residential customers or do we offer it to both residential and commercial. We have some customers that own the business that we cut, and we also do their homes. So, we're kind of confused as to how to handle this. Please give us your opinion. And, if we do offer this option, I was planning on sending an invoice showing their whole season amount, minus the 10% discount. Is this a good idea? Of course it says right on the statement that if they choose not to take the option, to just disregard the invoice and we will bill them monthly. Thanks so much, you guys have been a big help so far."

Steve: "Becca, you are not bothering us. This is what the forum is all about. Asking questions and giving answers!

What you are asking here makes me think of the old phrase, 'a dollar today is worth more than a dollar tomorrow.'

If you can get paid in full for the year's worth of lawn care service, I would jump on it. I have seen some lawn care business owners offer 10% off for prepay. I have seen some that didn't offer anything.

But if you want to experiment with this and offer a discount for the year, yea do it! That would be great. Then you don't have to track people down for payment. You are also guaranteed that working capital for the year.

How best to approach it? I would say talk to your customers and let them know you are offering this service and the discount for pre-pay. Once they are used to it one season, they will most likely jump on and do it year after year."

Chestin from http://www.lawncaremarketingmagic.com had some great insight into this topic as well. "Give your customers the option to prepay for your services. For example, let's say you have someone that's interested in signing a year long contract for services but instead of you sending them a monthly invoice, you give them the option of paying it all upfront in exchange for 2 months worth of services free.

Now, you obviously need to know your costs very well to know how much you can afford to give them, but by providing this type of incentive you'll get a number of customers that would be more than happy to avoid all the hassles associated with sending payment PLUS they get 2 months worth of services for free."

Richard of http://www.thelawnblog.com suggested "We offer a 5% discount on prepaid contracts. And about 30% of my clients prepay. It's all about the savings, who doesn't love to save money. From the company owner's point of view, it starts the revenue coming in a lot earlier."

Lastly Pat jumped in and said "We sent out it looking like an invoice but it listed all the services we have done for them in the past with the regular price then a prepay discount of 10% if they signed it and returned a check by a deadline date. It was just a good way to bring money into the company earlier to cover the spring costs. It worked very well to big response on it."

Here is another great post that discussed this topic as well in greater detail.
http://www.gophergraphics.com/forum/cgi-bin/ikonboard.cgi?
act=ST;f=8;t=3346

Neighborhood yard sale marketing idea.

Here is a marketing idea. Create a spring neighborhood yard sale. Have your house be the main area it starts from and ask other neighbors if they are interested in taking part.

You will be hosting the event and it will give you a great opportunity to meet new potential customers in your area.

You could then hand out these flyers in your area and post them up all over the place and attract others to your spring neighborhood yard sale.

You could also have a table that promote your lawn care business and possibly offer discounts that day if a customer signs up with you for a year's worth of lawn care.

Download a this FREE flyer template from the Gopher Lawn Care Forum
http://www.gophergraphics.com/forum/cgi-bin/ikonboard.cgi?
act=ST&f=8&t=7180

GopherHaul business book of the month of Feb – 08.

Rich Dad, Poor Dad

By: Robert Kiyosaki

One of our forum members Jared gave us a great review of the book. He said "I'll throw my two cents in here. Rich Dad Poor Dad was a great eye opener to me. It really taught me to look at money differently, also to see assets and liabilities for what they really are. If something you own takes money out of your pockets it is a liability. We're talking cars, boats, primary residences, anything you make payments on. It took me a while to understand what he was saying there. How could my home be a liability? Isn't that the American Dream... to own a home?? He also says that things that put money in your pocket are assets, such as a CASH FLOWING rental property, a website, etc.

I also think that Kiyosaki's stuff is a great ENTRY to real estate investing, kind of like Ron Legrand. It opens your eyes and gets you fired up as hell, but then what?

As far as people living paycheck to paycheck trying to start in investing I say why not? Now, I'm not saying to quit your day job, but there are plenty of ways to invest without your own money being involved. With a decent credit score and good job you can get HML's or Hard Money Loans. The interest rates are high (up to 20% in some cases) but most HMLs will loan you what you need to buy a flip and the money to fix it up. I would advise that you really learn your market before you try something like this. I would also advise you read read and read some more to prepare yourself. Like the lawn care business, you wouldn't just jump in and buy all the expensive equipment if you didn't have a grasp on how a business works right? Same thing applies to real estate.

I want to throw one more thing out there (if ya don't mind)... those BS shows on tv.. the flip this/that/yourmomma's house shows.. It ain't that easy! Those shows are mostly glam and BS. I actually filmed two flips from last year to show people what really happens in flipping houses on a daily basis. What sucks is those two houses were the houses we have the most problems on... really got beat up. Anyway, those shows are entertainment, period. My two cents.. keep the change!!"

Check out Jared's website at http://www.FLIPITBIG.com

Looking Good Lawn Service also gave us a review of the book, he said "the Rich dad poor dad series is an inspirational series, done to promote education reform as well as give you the ability to know what you are aiming for. Having read rich dad poor dad several times, it begins to take on a whole new meaning with what you rediscover, take notes from it. I usually can read the book within two days. I do recommend reading the following books in his series, cash flow quadrant and guide to investing. They provide a lot of good advise and general mindset to get you to where you need to start and that is to get educated and learn first. These books and others like it motivated me to go back to school to get another bachelors in business administration and management and get my MBA, I will be done with both in 2 years. Also, I am re-structuring my landscaping company as well. Motivation and open willingness to learn and never stop learning is one of the key points."

If you would like to share your insight and review of this book, please join our discussion here
http://www.gophergraphics.com/forum/cgi-bin/ikonboard.cgi?act=ST;f=1;t=7309

GopherHaul 23

Overview of GopherHaul

Episode #23

Original Air Date: March 10, 2008

In this episode we discussed.
- GopherHaul breaks the 700,000 view mark!
- New or old lawn care trucks?
- Starting a lawn care business with a car.
- Sample letter to property managers.
- Tracking your advertising.
- Are you answering your phone?
- What newspaper ads work best?
- Search engine optimization techniques.
- Should you offer free mowing for a referral?
- GopherHaul business book of the month.

GopherHaul breaks 700,000 views.

I was very happy to find that the views of GopherHaul broke the 700,000 view mark. That is just fantastic.

New or old lawn care trucks?

You don't need a new truck when you are starting your lawn care business. Check out Dave's truck as an example. From this post here

http://www.gophergraphics.com/forum/cgi-bin/ikonboard.cgi?
act=ST;f=4;t=7448

Dave wrote us about his truck. He said it is a "91 Mazda B2200 with the non-existent clutch. In the picture it's filled with 250kg (550lbs) of branches and debris from a rather large brush clearing job on a forested property.

It definitely helps to save on fuel...I usually spend around $40 per week on gas for it, with gas prices at $1.15/litre (~$4.37/gallon). I usually find that it doesn't affect my image too much, a lot of the guys around here are the individually-run Asian businesses, whose trucks tend to be a lot more beaten up than mine.

My only issues with it are the constant breakdowns. My starter failed twice last year (the first time I hit it with a hammer and it unseized), and it is almost certainly going to need a new clutch this year. This is the truck my boss started the company with 5 years ago, getting from his parents, and he's since bought the other two.

I remember seeing, on the forum, the guy with the green Escort and whatever you can make work when you're starting out is what I'd go for... There is no point taking on a bunch of unnecessary debt when you're starting out."

Brandon then offered his view on new trucks. He said "I buy all my vehicles used and cheap (less than 4k). I don't want more payments. My most often used truck is my 1976 F250 with a 460. Can't hurt it and if it breaks, I can fix it. I also have a newer Suburban that is my wifes, but we own it."

Tony then added "you don't need a BRAND new 35K or 45K truck right off the bat to get into the business, I currently have Chevy 2000 S10, that I bought for 6K with only 36K miles on it, but I got lucky although if I do build up and pick more business I do want to get a newer truck. I know someone now who just went out and bought, a newer truck + a brand new 7x14 trailer enclosed for $6900.00 and I think 2 new Exmark Lasers "not sure which ones" but he is getting into a lot of debt and I don't believe he even has any clients. Just as easy as it is to start your own lawn business it's all just as easy as going under."

So when you are out and about driving around during the day, thinking you need to have brand new equipment, think of what all these guys from the Gopher

Forum had to say about the issue and maybe you will feel more comfortable with an older truck that you own, instead of a new one you need to make payments on.

Starting a lawn care business with a car and a mower.

To take this concept a little further, a while back one of our Gopher Forum members, Landscape Warrior, told us his story on how he got his lawn care business started with a push mower and his car. That's right! He didn't even have a truck yet, which just goes to show you how you can get started with very little. At the time, Bill wrote us "I started in May 2007 on Craig list and my slogan was Your mower, my service! It worked ok and I got 3 customers. I was so  surprised it worked. So in June I changed from that to putting my mower and weed wacker in the back of my car. I now have 14 customers none on contracts. I feel like I can't ask for a lot due to the way I come across with no truck, just not very professional looking. I will be getting a truck next year. What do you think." from the our blog at http://lawnchat.com/?p=39

Here is the picture of Bill's set up that he posted in the Gopher Lawn Care forum.

2008 is definitely going to be a bigger for Bill and his lawn care business. He wrote in another post how he scaled up to a pickup truck. Bill wrote "Well i look a little more like a lawn care service now!!! I am the one that drove the green Ford Escort all of last year. I am looking around now for pricing on either magnets or just lettering for my windows haven't yet decided."

So let this be a great example of use what you got and get started today. ***Don't put off starting your business until the future sometime. There is no better time than the present.*** As we see with our friend Bill, he made his dream happened and you can too.

Join in on this discussion here http://www.gophergraphics.com/forum/cgi-bin/ikonboard.cgi?act=ST;f=4;t=7261

Sample letter to property managers.

Emerald Green Lawn Care was very kind enough this past month to share with us a letter they send to property managers in their area.

Many times in the Gopher Lawn Care Forum we will see the question be asked on how to get commercial jobs. Well, an important thing to know when you want to get commercial jobs, is find out when the property is put up for bid. A great way to find this out is by contacting the property management company and letting them know you exist and you want to be placed on their bid list.

Here is the letter that was sent to us. You could also send this out in an email as well.

"Baxxxx xxxx
Emerald Green Lawn Care

Miss Clarke,

Hello, please allow me to take a moment of your time. My name is Bxxxxx xxxx and I represent Emerald Green Lawn Care.

I would like to be considered for any and all Property Maintenance contracts or jobs that you may have coming up this year. My company is professionally licensed and insured.

We have been serving the Tri-Cities area for 10 years. You can speak to me at any time, and be confident knowing that your needs will be addressed immediately. We offer mowing, edging, planting, natural & permanent mulch, retaining walls, and have recently included hydroseeding, erosion control, and spray-on-mat.

Please add me to your bidders list and please contact me for any size job you may be considering. I am always happy to give free estimates. You can reach me at (423) ###-xxxx or emxxx@###

Sincerely,

Baxxx xxxx"

A big thank you to Emerald Green. If you have questions on using this letter, please feel free to join in on the post here.

http://www.gophergraphics.com/forum/cgi-bin/ikonboard.cgi?
act=ST;f=29;t=7403

Tracking your advertising?

When you first get started most of the time you really aren't too concerned about tracking your advertising, you are more focused on getting any job you can and surviving. However, as soon as you can though, it is very important for you and your business to track which advertisements are working for your lawn care business and which ones are not.

Let's jump to a post on the Gopher Lawn Care Forum. Kim posted a question **"How does everyone keep track of where your new customers got your number from so you can track your marketing profits and which ones to use again?**

I have to admit that last year when things got real busy I kinda slipped on this.

So my plan to fix it this year is to ad that info to each customers job jacket in their file. That will allow me to gather the info when time allows, so I can get a clear view for next year when planning my advertisement."

Now you may be asking yourself why is this question important? Well the simple reason why is you could be placing ads all over town and paying hundreds of dollars doing so and none of the ads may be working. In fact all of your advertising could be a complete waste of money. As we all know, you should never be pouring money down a drain, instead you should be making sure ever advertising dollar you spend comes back to you in the form of new customers and not only covers your advertising expenses, but makes you a nice profit as well.

I responded to Kim in the post by saying "My take is keep it really painfully simple or you won't keep up on this. When the season gets busy, it is easy to put this off and when the season slows down, you will be wishing you did keep track of it.

How do you keep it simple? Create a really simple spreadsheet. Print out the spread sheet. have it right near your phone and then just check off when someone calls you because they heard of you from the newspaper. Or they heard of you from a referral, or from a flyer. If you have different tracking codes, make sure you have them on your spread sheet. Then when you have time, take the count from your printout and enter it into your spread sheet and print a new blank spread sheet."

Kim then responded by saying "I was just reading something about putting **tracking codes on all your ads**. I think that using the easiest form is the best, will probably go with the spread sheet then try to ad to their job details when I have the time."

Now you may be wondering **what is a tracking code**? Say you create a lawn care flyer and you have some kind of offer like 10% a Spring yard clean up. Make sure in the coupon you include some kind of simple tracking code that you will know where the ad came from when the customer hands you the coupon. Keep it nice and simple! You can do this.

Chuck really had an eye opening experience once he started tracking his ads. Chuck said "I keep track of everything. I write the source (newspaper, phone book, word of mouth, walk up, online) on the top of my copy of an estimate or proposal because I always keep those. Two nights ago I sat down with my wife to crunch those numbers. My findings were surprising. About 65-70% of my business thus far has come from 1 source & at an advertising cost of just over $10 per customer! Pretty cheap. I tracked how many from each source. What was the average amount spent by the customers from each source too. Sometimes an add in one place will bring several small spenders & while another brings a few big money accounts. Different publications have a different type or class of readers!"

After hearing this from Chuck, I asked him "Now that you know this one ad is pulling that much of a response, what will you do now, knowing this information? How will this effect your marketing and business decisions?"

Chuck responded by saying "Of course it will affect future marketing, I have a new advertisement going into effect there asap. I can't believe we did so well with an ad I only ran for about a month & a half. I kick myself in the ass for not realizing it earlier."

Then our friend Justin posted a FREE Excel budget template spreadsheet in the post. You can download this and use it to help your lawn care business. You can download this template and join in on the discussion here

http://www.gophergraphics.com/forum/cgi-bin/ikonboard.cgi?
act=ST;f=8;t=7356

This conversation then led to another great one about the importance of answering your phone!

Are you answering your phone?

This is a trap many many lawn care businesses fall into. When they first get started, they tend to be one man operations and because they spend most of their day mowing lawns, they are not answering their business phone. As we will see, it is very important you have all your business calls forwarded to your cell phone and have it set on vibrate so you know when someone is calling, even when you are mowing.

Mike started of this post by asking "Anyone ever have any luck placing newspaper ads for lawn service?"

Chuck: "Worked pretty well for me. Keep it simple 3-4 lines. Then answer your phone or get somebody to do it for you. Too many lawn care operators place ads then they're out working all day & don't even return the calls the same day. If we don't answer we make sure to get back to them within 30 minutes (If they call the office my wife calls the cell phone & I check it between virtually every stop). Often times if you get there 1st to provide an estimate & you are professional, Courteous, & knowledgeable you can earn their business. If you wait to get back to them, somebody will beat you to it!"

He also had a great story to tell us how he learned of this importance of answering his phone that I wanted to share with you.

Chuck: "The only reason I know that to be a fact is that I was (& am a licensed health/life Insurance agent) just prior to starting my business. With the firm I worked for we specialized in affordable products for small business & the self employed. I spent days cold calling mom & pop shops from construction to pizza places, to landscapers, to painters & lawn care companies. I found it odd that I never got a hold of a single lawn care owner or manager on the 1st call. (& no my caller ID didn't say abc insurance co....)

Oddly, one did call me back & do business with me... during my appointment with him I admitted the hours in the insurance biz were crazy, 80+ hours most weeks & the cash was good but I had no life at all. I said I was contemplating starting a business of my own. Lawn care was already on my mind which is why

I said that to him, I was wondering what he would say. The guy said *"why don't you start a lawn care business?"There's a lot of competition but plenty of work & most of the competition out there is pretty lousy at what they do. I started mine 3 years ago & I make about 2k a week most weeks"*. Well we sat there shooting the breeze about it. That night was the first time I seriously ran the idea past my wife. We are now friendly competitors."

You can join this discussion by visiting the Gopher Lawn Care Forum here.

http://www.gophergraphics.com/forum/cgi-bin/ikonboard.cgi?
act=ST;f=29;t=7421;

What newspaper ads work best?

Isn't it amazing how one great discussion leads to another? All this talk about newspaper ads really got our minds rolling and our friend Keith, lawn care business author and owner of http://www.startalawncarebusiness.com , jumped in with a great post. In it he said "I think newspaper ads are still a very viable form of advertising. Wording and placement are key. If you give free estimates (and who doesn't?) definitely put **"FREE ESTIMATES"** in your ad. Also, if you do just one area of town, say so in your ad. This will focus your calls to a centralized geographic location.

I never liked the results I got from ads in the "services offered" section of the paper.

If your paper runs a "Business Classified" section, consider placing your ad there. It will cost more as you will probably have to run your ad for a month at a time. The cost might be as high as $250 depending on the number of subscribers.

I have always found the "Business Classified" section far superior to any other form of print advertising.

Once you place your ad, keep good records of the type of customers and revenue generated by the ads. If it works for you, keep at it."

WOW! I think we covered a lot of ground with all that great information! WHEW!

Search Engine Optimization (SEO)

What is search engine optimization or SEO for short? Well think of it as anything you can do with your lawn care business website to improve your ranking in search engines. This is very important and I will tell you why. If your website employees proper search engine optimization techniques, your website will then rank high when local customers look for local lawn care businesses to service their property. Keep in mind, this is **FREE ADVERTISING** for your lawn care business. Most people won't go beyond the first page when they do a search, so you want to appear in the top ten search engine results, ideally. Let's now take a look at this SEO technique Richard shared with us.

Our friend Richard of http://www.thelawnblog.com posted this great SEO idea. In his post, Richard said "Search engines also use postal addresses in the "about" or "contact " page to detect your default country. If you have a Google Map of your business location on your contact page, it can also help with Google Local or regional rankings. Even though the address element technically means "contact info for this web page", if you use an address element on your website, like the example below, Google will interpret it as a physical address.
  Code Sample

```
<address>
Business Name
Street Name
City Name
Zip code
Country Name
</address>
```

What will this do, or how can it help me?

Well most of us don't want global business or to be listed in Germany's Google. We want the lady 2 blocks away to find us. Anything that can help you rise in the rankings for local searches is what you need."

Richard also reminded us this isn't the only SEO technique you should employee "it doesn't replace any other forms of SEO just helps point google to your contact info easier."

Try this technique out in your lawn care business website html and let us know how it works out for you.

If you'd like to ask further questions on this post please visit the post here at the Gopher Lawn Care Forum.

http://www.gophergraphics.com/forum/cgi-bin/ikonboard.cgi?act=ST;f=6;t=7346;

Should you offer a FREE mowing for a referral?

Emerald Green Lawn Care created this mailer with a coupon and wanted to know what we thought of the idea of offering two free mowings when you refer a friend to his lawn care service. He explained his in the post, "I would just put them in with the invoices at the end of the month."

Now this actually turned out to be a very complicated discussion and we discussed it in great detail with our marketing guru Chestin of lawncaremarketingmagic.com.

Note: *If you would like to listen to the podcast, which is about an hour in length, visit our podcast directories here*

http://www.talkshoe.com/tc/15950

and here

http://odeo.com/channel/797663/view

and listen to the podcast from 02-28-08 with Chestin.

In the podcast, Chestin discussed how you shouldn't send out marketing material in your invoices that asks the customer to turn even more customers your way through a referral program. Why? Well as Chestin described it, he said when a customer has to write you a check for services, it is usually a painful experience. They just won't be in the mood to turn even more customers your way through your referral marketing offer.

Instead what you should consider doing is sending out a letter to your customers in a separate mailing and then make them an offer with your referral program.

Another great point Chestin made was, instead of offering them a free mowing when they turn a new customer your way, consider offer a gift certificate for say $50 at a local restaurant. You have to make sure the offer will work for you and seem to be believable for your customers. If the offer seems too good to be true, they may not bite. They will also not jump on the referral offer if it seems they are going to have to jump through hoops to get the offer you are presenting them.

If you are interested in joining this specific discussion or would like to download this coupon template and edit to your needs visit this post at

http://www.gophergraphics.com/forum/cgi-bin/ikonboard.cgi?
act=ST;f=8;t=7386

GopherHaul business book of the month.

March 2008

No Such Thing as Over-Exposure: Inside the Life and Celebrity of Donald Trump
by Robert Slater

If you love watching the Apprentice and want to learn more about the man behind it all, Donald Trump, this is a great book to read. This book really gives the reader an insiders point of view of the goings on in the Trump organization and how Donald conducts business.

Reading this book will no doubt expand your mind and make you rethink the ways you currently run your business.

Also if you are a big fan of reading business and entrepreneur books, check out my reading list at the Gopher Lawn Care Business Forum here.
http://www.gophergraphics.com/forum/cgi-bin/ikonboard.cgi?act=ST;f=1;t=792

I have listed years worth of the readings I have done. This list should keep you busy reading for quite some time.

GopherHaul 24

Overview of GopherHaul

Episode #24

Original Air Date: March 30, 2008

In this episode we discussed.
- Spotlight on a new forum member.
- The problem with telemarketing.
- How to buy a lawn care business.
- Advertising to buy lawn care accounts?
- How to sell lawn care accounts.
- Entrepreneur of the month.

Spotlight on a new forum member.

A new forum member joined up on the forum and gave us a little background on how he got started in the lawn care industry. Rob, wrote us "I decided to start the business when I couldn't find a job that I wanted to do over the summer. I didn't like being an umpire, and caddy at a golf course was just not for me. I called the grocery stores and you have to be 16. So I said "Well I'll just cut grass and get a real job next year" But now that I'm making a website and doing marketing and stuff, I really like it. And I wouldn't get to do that at a regular job. I'm just starting for the first time and I got my first customer the other day. Her husband has a back problem or something like that so I knew that I would have a sale for sure. And sure enough, I told her what I was doing, gave her my business card, and she was so impressed that I had actual business cards, that she signed a contract right there.

So as of now I only have 1 customer, but I'm working on some designs for flyers right now, and hope to have them out by next week. And if I can't get the flyers to bring in some business, I'm gonna be heading door to door. My equipment. hmmmm. Don't know if it deserves the name equipment. lol. But I have a Toro push mower (self propelled) a gas weed eater, an edger, a leaf blower, and a snow blower." Isn't this a great story! Also keep in mind Rob is 15 years old!

I asked Rob "Is anyone in your family an entrepreneur or are you the only one?

What do you think you attribute your ability to make all this happen to?"

Rob: "Neither of my parents are, but my aunt and cousin are. My aunt runs a Banquet Center, and my cousin runs a real estate office. I think my cousin is what inspires me because he has a nice house and he just got a Mercedes, and I know I can't have all that right now, but I'm working my way up there."

Steve: "What has been the best piece of advice he has given you up to this point?"

Rob: "Probably don't ever let anyone tell you, you cant do something. And this sounds corny, but its true, because people look at me and say yea right, like a 15 year old can run a business and it's hard to overcome that."

Isn't this an inspiring story? I definitely think so. Thank you so much Rob, for sharing your insight with us.

The problem with telemarketing.

A few shows back we talked about one lawn care business owner who was using an automated telemarketing machine to call out phone numbers in his area to promote his lawn care business. If you are going to utilize telemarketing for your business, make sure you check your phone number list and remove those numbers that are on the do not call list.

What happens if you don't? A lawn care company was fined *$45,000 in the state of Missouri. The investigation by the state was started by a single complaint from 1 person.* Check out this post and read the story here

http://www.gophergraphics.com/forum/cgi-bin/ikonboard.cgi?act=ST;f=8;t=7642

How to buy a lawn care business.

One of our fellow forum members, Michelle, asked a really great question that many people are curious to know. **How much is a lawn care business worth?** Is it better to buy an existing lawn care business or start one from scratch. Let's check out her question.

Michelle: "Hi there - this is my first post, although I have been lurking for a few weeks.

Over the last month or so, my husband and I have decided to start a lawn care business. He works FT, but needs a more flexible schedule since he is working on becoming a commercial hot air balloon pilot. We only need to replace his income with the lawn care, but some extra would be great (especially with 5 kids at home). I drive a school bus, and he would do the same in the winter, so that would pay the bills during winter. He has talked for years about wanting to mow in the summer, and I think now is the right time.

The plan WAS for me to get the business going by starting out specializing in edging only (an old friend did that years ago, and she was quite successful at it) and doing the work myself, since my husband still has to keep his job.

We would take on a few mowing jobs for my husband to do after work to get it going. Then, if we build up enough in edging to replace his income, we could add the mowing/maintenance service and try to get 60 or so weekly mowing customers.

Since I am not new to the business arena (having run my own specialty painting/faux finishing business for 7 years) I started networking with some business contacts.

I found out a friend of mine who owns a contracting business had purchased a used lawn care outfit a few years ago (truck, trailer, mowers, equipment, plow, yard vacuum, etc.) to supplement his services, and has decided to get out of it. He found that after the expense of paying someone to do the work, he doesn't make that much.

He's including the client list and will include marketing the business in a newsletter for 1 year to help me out, and will send any calls for business to me. The truck already has a nice logo, and I like the name of the business, so we would probably keep that.

I am currently waiting to hear back on cost, but he said it wouldn't be much since all the equipment is good, but used. He even said would take payments since we are friends.

Any words of caution, things I should look for, when considering jumping at this chance? Or, would I be better of starting from scratch, and keep going down the same road I was headed?"

Chuck: "Well the fact that the guy is willing to take payments implies that he is relatively confident you can make enough to make the payments, That is a plus. However if he said he's not making enough to make it worth his while, It's probably not enough for you either. He may be under priced, or be managing it poorly, you need to find out which! If he's under priced, and you buy the business & jack up the rates you may lose a good percentage of his current customers. Are his current customers paying per service or contracted monthly?

A big unknown here is the cost like you said, So it's impossible to even weigh out until you know the cost, how much equipment & what it's worth, how many customers & what type of customers he has currently. You said a plow is included but you said you want extra income in the summer only. So....

1. It's equipment you don't need or want as you'll be driving a school bus.
2. Does he include plowing in the winter time for the current customers? Would you be locked into having to provide those services like it or not?

I looked at other businesses for sale too and ultimately decided to start from scratch with no loan over my head. But then again I had to start from customer #1 & build it up. Luckily you are just looking to supplement your income. But I'll tell you, get licensed & insured! My line trimmer threw a rock through a plate glass window last week. Stuff happens!"

Michelle: "Well, based on your response, I guess I wasn't too clear on a couple things...

This guy has financial figures for the business and it grosses about $80-100K annually, but he just manages the business. He pays a crew to do the actual work for about $40/hr, which really cuts into his pocketed profits. Not only is there the $40/hr, but the extra insurance (work comp, liability, etc), cost for payroll services, extra uniforms, etc. He told me and I agree with him, that if we are running the business and doing the work ourselves, we could make some good money.

He has a contracting business which is his bread and butter, and he was looking to fill a void in his services to realtors, mostly, in maintaining properties for sale. He said his crew of 3 people runs 40+ hours/week, but yes, I do need to know what he is charging on each job.

I think, too, with us just focusing on the business of lawn care as our sole business, we could bring more work in. We do have some people who are interested in working as independent contractors for us (meaning we don't have to take out taxes or pay work comp), or on a referral basis.

The problem with the realtor gig is you get customers that are not long term...but if you have a relationship with the realtor, you can put together a "welcome to the neighborhood deal" for the new buyer to try to keep them as a client since you already know "the lay of the land" so to speak.

My husband has wanted to plow snow for a few years now. We have an ATV with a plow, but he has wanted a plow for his truck. Yes, we would offer the plowing (husband would do that part) if they are accustomed to that, but we also know larger contractors always in need of drivers with plows on their trucks and they pay $70/hr. The school bus thing in the winter is just 3.5 hours/day, and as a sub driver, you work when you can, not necessarily every day.

Other than that, as far as the equipment goes, I think we would/could use everything he has, or if not, sell some of it. I guess the price is going to be what would make or break the deal for us. There is more included in this deal than we would have planned to purchase up front to get started, but if the price is right...

Yes, at this point, we are supplementing our income, but my husband is miserable at his job, so we would love to replace it asap (by April or May would be great), so I am thinking the built-in clientele is a good deal for us.

You bring up some very good points to think about (value of equipment, services currently offered to customers, how he charges, etc.).

THANK YOU for your response!!!"

Chuck: "No problem at all, I wish you luck with whichever way you go.
I know the business I looked at had about 10k (used value) in equipment, plus
about 130 per cut customers & no contracted customers. I decided against it
because he wanted $60k for the biz & I thought well many customers are loyal
to a guy who's been servicing them so long, but still when a new owner comes in
I figured it was fair to guestimate I might lose 10-15% just because I wouldn't be
the same guy they were used to.

I also knew most companies on average get lazy & do a lousy job & or become
unreliable. So I figured that I could build my business from the ground up by
doing a great job every time, offering competitive rates & better service. That's
what I've done so far & it's working for me. I was able to buy most of the
equipment with some cash from savings (used trailer, new trimmers, edgers,
blowers, chain saws, pole saw & hedge trimmer) & financed what I couldn't
being a new commercial mower. So instead of 60k overhead I only have about
1/8 of that debt & in less than a year my business is about half what his was
already. Every situation is different & like I said I wish all the best of luck to
you!"

This question reminded me of an older discussion I had with lawn care business
author Joel LaRusic, who discussed this topic in detail in a podcast interview I
had with him.

Note: You can listen to all my podcasts here
http://www.talkshoe.com/tc/15950

and here

http://odeo.com/channel/797663/view

In the discussion Joel said "*General rule of thumb for buying customers is that
they are worth about 1 month revenue. If they are commercial you'll pay a little
more and if there is a signed multi-year agreement in place then this will push
the price up too. So it could be worth as much as 2 or 3 months revenue
depending on the situation.*"

You can also read more on this topic in a blog post I made here
http://lawnchat.com/?p=51

Michelle: "Well, I think we have some ballpark numbers...about $15-20K for equipment, plus the business itself. Of course, he offered to do a contracted deal where we pay him a percentage of the business income after the first year, and just purchase equipment up front. (I trust this, as I have known this guy for about 6 years). Still, not a bad deal. He's calling me back today or tomorrow with some final numbers, so if they are right, we may consider - but at $15-20K, plus customers, I don't think we can do it.

On the other hand, the more we have thought about it, and like my husband has said, we could build it up and have no overhead, and buy equipment we need as we go. Yes, it may take a little longer, but we won't have that big up front expense. The whole business isn't a bad deal - at all, but I just don't think it's in our budget right now.

Thank you so much to everyone for all the input. Can you tell, I am still on the fence a little?

So, at this point, I think we are back to the original plan...I will push the lawn edging to start, and do that myself, then we'll add a lawn care division for my husband to run, starting weekends and evenings this year, and go for full time with both next year - anyone here doing strictly edging?"

Ultimately the discussion ended when I said to Michelle, if she felt more comfortable starting from scratch and learning as she went, that might be a lot easier for her and her husband.

You can join in on the discussion here,
http://www.gophergraphics.com/forum/cgi-bin/ikonboard.cgi?act=ST;f=29;t=7525

Advertising to buy lawn care accounts?

A real quick way to grow your business is to advertise that you are looking to purchase lawn care customer accounts. That is exactly what Fernando did when he made this post on craigslist.com

Fernando: "Hi, everybody!
Well I started using cragislist.com last month and so far I've gained 4 new accounts, (so I guess it works for me), but how many here use or have used this site?"

> Here is the text of the ad he place in craigslist. "Lawn Care Service LLC, offering top quality-professional job to your accounts. This is an upcoming Lawn Care Service Business owned and operated by a Self-motivated, Hard Working Gentleman, going on the second season this year, so I'm planning to expand my clientele this year by serving CENTRAL BREVARD County.
> -Too Tired over the Summer? …or can't keep up during the hot season?
> -Too Hard to work from Sunrise to Sundown?
> -Too busy to take care of ALL of your accounts during the "Crunch Time"?
> -Customers complaining about not cutting the lawn on time?
>
> **I am willing to buy Lawn Accounts**, and the best part of all is that your customers are going to be happy to know that you want to "Take Care" of their lawn by "referring" ME as their new Lawn Care Provider. It's a win-win situation for all of us, your Customer will be happy by having a reliable, on-time, quality job LCO, and You by having more time to spend time with your love ones.
> For more information or set up a meeting call me."

It is free to place these ads in craigslist and so far Fernando is gaining new clients through the site so good for him! Maybe this will inspire you to try this advertising technique out as well.

If you would like to join in on this discussion visit the post here
http://www.gophergraphics.com/forum/cgi-bin/ikonboard.cgi?act=ST;f=8;t=7521;

How to sell lawn care accounts.

We have been talking a lot about buying lawn care accounts, but what if you want to sell them? That is exactly what one of our forum members wanted to do when he made this post.

Greenmind wrote "I wanted to ask some of you guys what is the best way to sell my accounts. I have only about 20 accounts left to get rid of and I also have some equipment left. I have 8 weekly accounts and 12 bi-weekly accounts. These accounts produce about 20K per year. They are not on a yearly contract and I have had most for almost a year now. These also produced about 6K in extra business last year in pine straw, mulch and landscaping projects. I have them posted on craigslist as of yesterday and already have 7 responses to these accounts already! I also have a 6X12 black ramp gate trailer with wood floors and no rust. Also my trailer has a detached 6 ft. open basket and lock. The mower is a Toro Proline 37 in floating deck with a 14 hp Kohler engine, attached is a new Jungle Jims Two wheel sulkey. I just have over $200 dollars worth of service done at my local shop. I want to sell all these accounts and equipment for $5,500 dollars. I figured my mower and trailer are worth 2k and my accounts are worth $3,500. I got those numbers based on the monthly income plus the extras that came in last year. What do you guys think? Any experience with this? What is the best method?

My next question is I have not spoken to my customers about this yet. It is a decision I am reluctant to make. I got a job offer I cannot refuse at a time where my wife is pregnant and we have some debt we need to pay. I want to meet with my customers and the LCO and establish a good partnership between the new operator and my customers. My customers all pay on time and have been dependable."

Mike: "I bought out a total of 3 lawn care businesses when I had my first lawn business.

We agreed on the price, I paid the money, we wrote letters to the customers, took good care of them, and we never had a problem.

Thinking back I probably should have had a no compete with the former owner."

Greenmind: "My main concern is my customers not knowing the new owner of the company, and being upset. Should I talk to them first or just send them a

letter. I just want to do it professionally, that's all.
Do I need to personally introduce each customer to the new LCO?
Or is a letter enough. None of my customer have a contract so how does that effect the transfer process?

My main question for you is when you sent the letter, nobody called you and complained about switching service companies?"

Mike: "No, I didn't get any complaints most customers just want someone dependable, honest, and hard working.

I'm curious how you are arriving at your "buyout" price?

Have you checked some of his accounts to make sure they are priced in accordance with what you would charge?

One of the lawn companies I bought out was considerably higher in pricing than mine, so I ended up raising all my original customers up to that standard.

I'd be sure to get a non-compete contract with him. I got very lucky that I never had one, never needed one, but it's a good idea.

Just use some due diligence and you should be fine, let me know how it goes.

None of my customers were on contracts at that time residential contracts were not very common. It just makes you work a "little" harder with the new ones you bought. I did lose a few here and there, but I only paid 2.5 times the mowing price, and usually got at least 3 mows before they quit me."

If you would like to join this discussion, visit the Gopher Lawn Care Forum here
http://www.gophergraphics.com/forum/cgi-bin/ikonboard.cgi?act=ST;f=34;t=7567

Entrepreneur of the month.

Al Copeland. (Feb. 2, 1944 – Mar. 23, 2008)

Al Copeland was an amazing entrepreneur. He sold his car to buy into a donut franchise his brother owned. Then when a KFC opened nearby, he was amazed at the volume of traffic they had so he decided to start his own chicken restaurant which failed. He played around with the ingredients and spices and reopened Popeyes Chicken. Which he was able to grow to over 800 restaurants. Don't ever give up! Keep trying and experimenting.

If you get a chance, please do an internet search on this amazing entrepreneur. Remember you may not hit the big idea on your first try but as you go and experiment, you will learn more and more how to make things happen and this will improve your chances of success.

GopherHaul 25

Overview of GopherHaul

Episode #25

Original Air Date: April 20, 2008

In this episode we discussed.
- GopherHaul reaches 900,000 view.
- Need help selling my lawn care accounts.
- Podcast with author Ken LaVoie.
- Lawn care postcard review.
- Tips on buying used lawn care equipment.
- Lawn care marketing flyer.
- GopherHaul business book of the month.

GopherHaul reaches 900,000 views!

We are getting very close to the 1,000,000 view mark. This is getting very exciting!

I need help selling my lawn care accounts!

Greenmind wrote us "I am selling my accounts this week to a local landscaper. He wants to pay me in 3 payments. Over a 3 month period or 90 days as people stay with the new company. Also he does not want to pay the initial payment until all customers are contacted. Is he buying my business or my customers? Also is the 90 day period normal or am I being to generous, I have talked with several people and they seem to think that he is taking some risk by buying my accounts and thats part of the business and some suggest that I charge more for letting him pay over 90 days.

What do you guys think? Any help with someone with experience in this area would be very helpful. I don't want to get taken on this transaction. I worked very hard to get and keep these customers."

Steve: "I don't like this deal very much for you. There is a lot that can go wrong with it and I have seen plenty of businesses sold on payment terms that never get paid.

I would say you should get whatever payment you are looking to get all at once."

Dave: "If you are going to let him pay in installments, make sure that the payment amounts and deadlines are clearly written in a signed contract. Also, I would make sure that you contact the customers themselves...that way he can't claim that they left him when they really didn't. Whatever you do, make sure it's clearly documented, in case you need to take it up with him in court later."

Brandon: "I think the 90 days could be your potential problem in this deal. Have you checked this guys credit report? That should tell you a lot. If he has spotless credit, then you may be okay with doing it. Otherwise you may be able to take some collateral until he has paid up, like a lien on his truck, etc."

Get involved with this post here:
http://www.gophergraphics.com/forum/cgi-bin/ikonboard.cgi?act=ST;f=28;t=7823;

Podcast with author Ken LaVoie.

I had a great podcast interview with lawn care business Author Ken LaVoie. Of lawnguru.net. Ken wrote the book "How to Start a Lawn Care Business a Whole new way!"

1. We talked about the pitfalls of buying too much new too soon, Ken calls this 'Iron Addiction.'

2. How ego effects business decisions and how to control it.

3. Then we talked about what marketing ideas work and what don't.

4. When and how you should integrate your first employee into your business.

5. And this was a fantastic topic Finance, Debt and Growth - "The 50/50 Rule and stay in the black with the 20% Rule!" If you find yourself making a lot of money but at the end of the year wondering where it all went, it's very possible you are growing too fast. In Ken's 50/50 rule, he suggests not financing any more than 50% of the equipment price. If you need to finance more than that, you shouldn't be purchasing the equipment.

One of the things I was amazed with when talking with Ken was how the one type of marketing that worked best for him was word of mouth and nothing else he ever did worked as well as that. He has been doing this for 20 years too.

Early on Ken was mowing part time and working as a chef in a restaurant. When he had a disagreement with his boss and was fired, he found himself having to make his part time mowing into a full time job. The first thing he did was put an ad in the newspaper and then he was off and running. He said the newspaper ads tended to get a lot of price shoppers but to get himself going, this was all he needed. Later he got a small ad in the yellow pages and that seemed to bring in more profitable customers.

Tim had a great response to the podcast, he said "Well this is a forum and it is open for discussion, so here's my commentary. In the first ten minutes that I listened to, if you check out the previous post I submitted in Dec 2007 you will find I had made a post on the new vs used equipment, (keeping up with the JONES) the 20% growth rate but I posted 25%, also the first guy that called in is exactly right if you purchase any NEW equipment there better be 40% revenue over and above the cost of such equipment.

Example: If you want to buy a $10k mower there better be $28K just to cover that mower. This is basic business 101. I will say this again if you can't do the book keeping yourself then hire a CPA or at the very least a good book keeper and they will tell you if you can afford a new piece of equipment from your revenue to debit reports. Just because you have that one big contract and you think your on the highway to big money, doesn't mean you can afford it, to many unpredictable things can happen at any given time.

MOST of all, your business should never rest on any one customer being over 20% of your business. If you have all your business or over 50% depending on the revenue generated by one client you are headed for disaster. You better start working harder on getting more customers to balance your business better.

HINT: we have a projection of 200k + in revenue this year (2008) and not one customer totals more than 20% of that revenue. BTW April 1st was our 1 yr date. this is only our second season and we survived the worst drought in 30yrs, most didn't.

How did we? by not putting all our eggs in one basket, buying new trucks and equipment, I bought used mowers and when we generated enough to buy more I did but **only when I had 2 times the cost of that equipment**, We just bought a NEW Super Z 72" got it for almost 11k and its paid for, we own it! Last year we wrote off over 8k in bad debit to add to the unpredictable things that can happen. So think long and hard, think of all the bad things that could happen before you jump and start having big equipment payments.

I do not agree with the low-balling, doing it for 10 dollars less just to get the job kind of guy, I don't agree with the grab what ever you can theory, nor do I agree with the picking only certain types of customers to market. I was burned by a very upper class family and once by a department President of a large corporation. When the family broke up and the President was FIRED! So that theory goes right out the door for me.

I have been and will continue to provide excellent service at a fair and reasonable rate and I will let the client decide if they can afford it. I was surprised once by the looks of a property, when the man handed me 10 k in cash before I even started and when I completed, he paid that day in cash. Now this client never appeared to have 2 nickles, but looks are deceiving in all neighborhoods. Think about it, don't limit yourself, and always protect yourself in some way, shape or form."

Join our discussion on this podcast and listen to it here
http://www.gophergraphics.com/forum/cgi-bin/ikonboard.cgi?act=ST;f=22;t=7744

Lawn care postcard review.

Chuck posted a post card design he was considering sending out and said "Here's what I've been contemplating sending out. I know I have no fancy logo or nice looking lawn photos on it but I can't fit them with all the text I'd like on it."

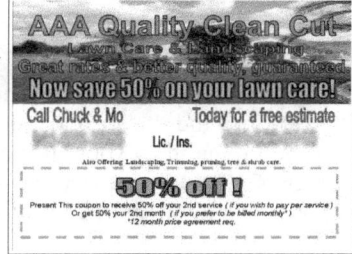

He asked everyone to give him a review of his lawn care marketing material and we got a lot of great responses. If you would like us to review your marketing material, please feel free to make a post and include it.

Jon: "1) The offer: I think both offers on there are fine, because it's actually 1 offer with 2 options, options are good, and you are K.I.S. (I will leave the "stupid" out), you are keeping it simple with just 1 offer and 2 options, it would be different if it were 1 offer with like 5+ options, that would be confusing.

2) "FREE", If you are going to use that word, I as a consumer will be expecting something FREE, if I get a piece of marketing material and it says FREE really large to get my attention but I don't see anything free, then I will be pissed that the advertiser "conned" me into reading their offer, and I lose respect for the company…Unless you are going to say "FREE" to read this advertisement", don't do it, you don't see free nowhere on my website, well, yes you do, for the shipping, and why, because it IS FREE.

3) Regarding the artwork, thanks Rich for mentioning the 300dpi. Don't take this the wrong way Chuck, not everyone is a graphic designer, so when someone with limited experience or resources attempts to design their own piece, you can usually tell, unlike having it done by an "actual" Graphic Designer…in this case you can tell it is done by someone with limited experience, for one I would use an image related to lawn care, the image you have on there is stretched. Be careful on how you put text in front of an image, this is where using a Graphic Designer comes in."

Chestin from lawncaremarketingmagic.com offered this review: "Wow, I wish I'd seen this post earlier because it's a great discussion on a subject

I LOVE talking about, so forgive me if I get a bit long-winded here.

First off, don't be afraid of lots of text. Yes, people are in a hurry BUT if you have an offer that appeals to them, makes their life easier, solves their problems, etc., they'll read it.

Plus, you're trying to get them to spend money. Why in the world would they want to make the decision to spend money with you after reading just a few lines of text? If they didn't care about quality, customer service, or any of the other things you're building your business on, it isn't going to matter what you say other than '**CHEAP**'. You can't convey the things that set you apart from your competition in a few short lines of text.

When you go to meet a new customer, perform an estimate, and ultimately sell them, do you limit yourself to less than 200 words? Of course not. You're going to say as much as you need to say in order to convince your prospect that you're the best person for the job because of X,Y, and Z.

And even though your postcard is only trying to convince people to pick up the phone and call, your challenge is still the same. When you limit your postcard (or sales letter, or flyer, or door hanger, etc.), you're severely limiting your chances of actually getting a call.

So again, **DON'T BE AFRAID OF A LOT OF TEXT**. I know this will rankle quite a few people here, but studies have shown again and again that when trying to sell a service (like lawn care), more text pulls better than less text.

1. **Replace the name of your company with an attention grabbing headline.** When you use your company name as the headline, it becomes a 'deadline'. You have 2 seconds to convince your prospect to read the rest of your postcard and you won't do that with your name. Try something like, 'Save 50% On Your Year Round Lawn Care' or something else that immediately conveys the main benefits of your offer.

2. **Translate your various services into benefits.** What benefits will they get as a result of these services?

3. You've already presented a good offer, but consider rewording it to **make it a little less confusing**.

4. As you already mentioned, **include a deadline to create some sense of urgency**. This will help motivate your prospects to pick up the phone RIGHT NOW instead of sticking it up on the fridge or in a drawer, only to be forgotten.

5. If you can, **include a testimonial** from one of your satisfied clients. This helps reinforce your message and offer."

You can join in on this discussion here.
http://www.gophergraphics.com/forum/cgi-bin/ikonboard.cgi?
act=ST;f=8;t=7623

and

http://lawnchat.com/?p=134

Tips on buying used lawn care equipment.

Chuck, a member of the Gopher <u>Lawn Care Forum</u> asked a great question today I wanted to pass on to everyone. He asked:

"I came across this in my local area on craigslist....is 3000 hrs alot for a diesel mower? I know it is for a gas machine but I don't know.."?

Tim: "I would have to say it is very close to rebuild time. As you know **gas will last about 2100 hours** before you replace or rebuild and that depends on how it is taken care of, proper maintenance is the key, A **diesel will last about 2 times what gas will** if it is taken care of, and serviced properly, so if it has 3000 hrs and life expectancy is only 4000 then it is close. If the price is right and the deck is still in good shape, no welds and good pulleys and bearings and not much work is needed then its up to you at that point. If it is a Kabota engine then you may, depends again on care of the machine, get about 5000 hrs and then you're still over half way to rebuild time. I'm not big on grasshoppers but to each their own. Remember that diesel machines take more maintenance all the way around."

Join this discussion further here
http://www.gophergraphics.com/forum/cgi-bin/ikonboard.cgi?
act=ST;f=28;t=7791

and here

http://lawnchat.com/?p=130

Free lawn care marketing flyer.

Chestin of http://www.lawncaremarketingmagic.com gave us a lot of great lawn care marketing tips this episode and to further illustrate how important it is to create a great flyer, he even posted a flyer you can download and edit to use with your own lawn care business. Thanks Chestin!

Visit this post to join the discussion and download the Free lawn care flyer template.
http://www.gophergraphics.com/forum/cgi-bin/ikonboard.cgi?act=ST;f=8;t=7521

GopherHaul business book of the month.

May 2008

Think Big and Kick Ass by Donald Trump.

At first I wasn't going to get this book because I have read a bunch of books already by Donald, but I gotta say, this one is his best ones yet. What I like most about it is his personal stories and how he dealt with different issues that arose in his life.

If you get a chance, read this book.

GopherHaul 26

Overview of GopherHaul Episode #26

Original Air Date: May 10, 2008

In this episode we discussed.
- GopherHaul reaches 1,000,000 views.
- Should a new lawn care business advertise in the phone book?
- New 1 – on – 1 private consulting forum added.
- Is it too late to start your lawn care business?
- How much should I pay new employees?
- GopherHaul business book of the month.
- Quote cards and cross marketing.
- Referral marketing tip.

GopherHaul reaches 1,000,000 views!

Hurray!!! We finally did it. GopherHaul broke the 1,000,000 view ceiling.

Should a new lawn care business place an ad in the phone book?

When you are just getting started with your lawn care business should you be advertising in the yellow pages? This is a question our friend Matt asked.

Matt: "I had thought about advertising in the phone book.

Newspaper advertising is $153 a month for a 1 x 1 1/2, no contract.

Yellow Book advertising is $101 a month for a 4 x 4, plus another placement in the book, but they want a years contract.

He (yellow pages ad salesman) said I would save money using Yellow Book(Phone Book)

Also people are looking on the web for services.

If any of you advertise in the phone book, how good is the response? The sales man told me if you are looking to stay busy, and the phone to ring off the hook this is the way to go. Which I know he is just trying to make a sale.

He had also mentioned that I have to pay 2 payments up front and nothing until Jan of 2009 until the ad starts, cause this years book (2008) is already out and they are getting ready for the 2009 books."

Steve: "Yellow pages is something you can do after you are in business for a few years. I am sure it will bring in some customers but signing an annual contract for the yellow pages when you are starting out and trying to conserve funds I don't think is the best way to spend advertising dollars. I would do more short run ads and then work the neighborhood you are servicing to help broaden your customer base and tighten your routes."

James: "A friend of mine placed a half page ad in the yellow pages... His results... 90% of the calls were from retired persons and lower income areas, which kinda makes sense.... now the way the internet is, it's faster to find information on a laptop than opening the phone book. I really think your money would be spent elsewhere."

Matt: "Yeah, advertising in the yellow pages sounds good and all, but as Steve said I don't really think it is quite time for me to do that adventure yet.

That is what I have noticed from my website and what I have heard is that people are looking businesses and services up on the internet now a days.

I had thought about doing flyers or door hangers sometime and taping them on the mailboxes or do direct mailings. Probably cheaper to do flyers on mailboxes as long as I don't open the mailbox.

Whenever I am servicing a yard in the neighborhood, if I have time in between stops. I walk that same road and put business cards on doors of homes, then I drive by a day or so later and see if the business cards are gone off the doors, 100% of the time they are gone."

This is a really great discussion. New start up businesses need to make sure their advertising dollar works as fast as possible. Business cards, flyers, door hangers, all of these things tend to bring you customers quicker than locking yourself into a long term advertising contract with a phone book. Stick with quick base hits when you are getting started.

If you'd like to join in this discussion further, join it here.

http://www.gophergraphics.com/forum/cgi-bin/ikonboard.cgi?act=ST;f=8;t=7955;

New 1-on-1 private lawn care business consulting forum added.

I just added a new section to the Gopher Lawn Care Business Forum. This section will fill a gap that I have seen for quite some time. I have met a few very talented businessmen and lawn care business authors who are able to assist in answering questions on the forum. However they were not able to dedicate the amount of time that they could have because of other commitments. So I asked them, if we set up a private forum area where a reader paid a subscription fee of $19.95 a month to get 1-on-1 business consulting advice, would they be able to make time to assist the forum readers? They both agreed, so lucky for us, we now have access to tap into their insights and thoughts for business advice. If you are running a lawn care business and are in need of business advice that will put you ahead of your competition by leaps and bounds all for less than the price of mowing one lawn per month, we have a great service for you. To sign up, either visit the Gopher Lawn Care Business Forum or visit Keith's site at http://www.startalawncarebusiness.com or visit Ken's website at http://www.lawnguru.net and you can sign up for a subscription from either lawn care business expert.

Is it too late to start your lawn care business?

One of our new forum members made a post asking if it was too late for him to start his lawn care business. We got quite a few great responses to this question and ultimately came to the conclusion that it is never too late to get started.

Eric: "I'm just getting my business started but it's already May so everyone seems to have a company all ready so what should I do for this season?"

Chuck: "I don't know where you are located but I started my business in mid June.... Well I started advertising, then did a bunch of estimates & when I started to get work scheduled I went out & bought equipment. I was literally going "yes I can trim you hedges Sir" Note to self: buy a hedge trimmer. My first invoice wasn't til like June 20th! Not an ideal time to start but it can be done."

Eric2: It's never too late to get contracts. In fact, as the weather gets hotter, you'll find more and more customers looking to hire out that weekly task. If you want to work, go around and pick out businesses or homes you'd like to maintain. Look over the property and submit an unsolicited proposal with all the services costs and payment options. It's not OK to trespass on the property, just look at it from the street. Mail the proposal printed on high quality paper & envelope. Use spell check, and proper format.

In my area, I have the ability to use the online county tax record to discover the owners name by the street address. Even though I've never met the owners, I can personalize the quote. Make notes of what problems you could see, and provide your solutions and costs.

Don't expect a high percentage of replies after the first mailing. Your initial effort to record the names & addresses should be entered into a database so you can send out consistent and reoccurring letters. If you start to perform work for a neighbor, mention that name and location. The people on the fence can drive by and check your work. Or you could photograph that property and send it around. Compliment & thank your paying customers publicly and in person. Don't just take the money and run."

Keith from startalawncarebusiness.com: "I remember my very first large commercial property a few months after I started my business. It was about 2 acres and I still only had my starter 22" push lawn mower. Luckily, I already had a trailer.

I made the lawn cutting agreement Tuesday afternoon. By Wednesday morning I had found and bought my first Snapper commercial walk behind mower (used). I was on the job by 10:00AM Wednesday. I barely even knew how to operate it at that point.

Eric, it is never too early or too late to get jobs. Starting out, you can't be too picky on the types of jobs you will be hired to do. How are those two spring cleanup estimates coming along...did you get the jobs? If you do great work they will very likely turn into more than one time jobs. Remind each person you work for that you are looking to add customers.

Today is Saturday and it's not even noon yet. If you hustle, work your butt off, and each of your estimates recommends you to two other customers, you can have 4 steady customers by day's end."

Brandon: "I also started in June. I bought some business cards online, then went knocking on doors. I left my cards at the doors where no one was home. The next day, my second call was from a man who ran a property management company who found my card when he got home from work. I told him I had been in business for a while (like maybe 2 days). He asked me if I had insurance...of course (just like above, note to self..buy insurance). By the end of the week, he had me on 6 accounts, 2 were commercial. They continue to send me work all the time because they like my work ethic.

Its never too late to start, maybe just a little to HOT!"

Fernando: "LOL! same story here. I started on April 1st last year and I have a base of 12 accounts.

**Can you install SOD? --"SURE!", that day I stayed up like around 2am learning how to install SOD, hehehe, it was a small project, this is pretty bad and risky at the same time, but isn't this what a "Rebel/Outlaw/Entrepreneur" does?

Keep on fighting!"

Aaron and Nicole: "I SO did the same thing on a few. Yeah I can trim your 120 feet of hedges no problem. Note to self. 17" 5 year old hedge trimmers are not gonna cut it.

Oh, yeah I can take care of those second floor gutters. Um.. 6 foot ladder.. problem. Need a ladder. Check!

I ended up picking up one at Sam's club. It's a 19 foot articulated ladder. Really cool but I realized it is not going to work for 2 story houses with a crawl space. Just not tall enough. Well, turns out my 4th client has a 19 foot ladder and 28 foot extension ladder he does not need anymore. Offered to sell to me $25 each. He even told me I can just come by and borrow them whenever I need to until I have a place to put them. So, I took back the one from Sam's club and will be using his ladders until I get into a truck with a ladder rack that I can lock them up on. It wouldn't make much sense to strap them to my 95 Ford Aerostar for an extended period of time."

Eric: "Thank you for all your help I really thought it was too late but I guess I was wrong! I've been watching a good friend of mine who owns a landscaping business for my entire life mow and and do all the landscaping then this year I asked him for a job but he said he couldn't give me one till I was 18 so I was like screw this I'll go out and open my own landscaping company and here I am!"

Steve: "Eric, with your experience now of starting your lawn care business mid-season, do you have any advice you could share with others who find themselves in a similar situation?"

Eric: "I think the advice I would give anyone trying to start up in mid May is that all you need is to get your name out there and have a little patience since there aren't going to be as many people out there looking for you but there are still the people who have not realized that the lawn needs to be cut. I recommend the flyers that you have provided on your forum, the one with the light switch worked the best for me. I also purchased t-shirts and signs for the truck so that also helped but the biggest advice is just to go out and do it. I wouldn't have been able to do it without this forum and this website so thank all of you guys."

There you have it. As we have seen in this discussion, many new lawn care businesses were started mid-season and many of the owners learned as they went. Don't put off starting your business until the next year. Who knows if that next year will ever come.

Join this discussion further here.
http://www.gophergraphics.com/forum/cgi-bin/ikonboard.cgi?act=ST;f=29;t=7961

Question on hiring. How much should I pay?

Chuck started off this discussion by asking "I am interviewing now to hire my 1st helper. It will be all legit. of course, taxes, comp. yada yada yada.....

I posted an ad on craigslist about the position. 2-3 days a week to start. Pay based on experience.

I knew things were bad in the economy, but I've got guys calling that live an hour plus away, begging for the job. I'm getting.... "please, I've done this some before & I'll take minimum wage to start if you want, just give me a chance?!"

I've never been big on paying minimum wage to anyone.... It seems to me that says your not worth anything & if I could pay you less I would..... I was just wondering what the average new wage for the industry is?

Thanks guys this should be interesting I think."

Eric: "I think you'll find there's a very good reason they don't already have a FT job. Part of my hiring process meant the candidate had to provide a recent copy of their DMV record. I'd rather see that before my insurance company pulled it and rejected the guy as a driver. We also had them sign permission for a criminal records check due to our government contracting.

One of my residential customers was head of security on base. If I had a questionable candidate, it was a simple process to add him to the list for approval and records check.

During the interview phase I'd ask the guy to do simple tasks to determine his level of experience and/or knowledge. The tasks were tailored to what he said on his resume or application. For example, a heavy equipment operator should be well versed in changing the grease tube in a grease gun. So I'd hand them the gun and watch which end he wanted to start with.

Chainsaw operator better know all the parts of the saw, how to clean the air filter, and especially how to sharpen by hand. I can't tell you how many times I'd have to personally sharpen a saw or just get it started. Tree men needs to show me knots in the climbing rope and belt hook-up. Also need to show me tie off of the groundsman tag line for limbing.

Mowing crew needs to identify which engines must be fueled with mixed gas and what ratio. Show me how to reload a weed eater string head. Start up the walk behind after checking the oil and drive it around. Mow my front yard the right way with a pusher.

I heard a lot of stories. If I offered a job it would be an "at-will" contract. This means they could quit or be fired without reason. I'd tell every one of them not to discuss their pay rate with anyone else in the company. Their rate was between me and them. The job duties and difficulty were explained up front. Don't get the idea that after working one or two weeks you need to come ask for a raise because the hours are long and the work is physical. Raises are based on performance and profits, not whining. Steps up the ladder to foremen are based on skills, common sense, and responsibility."

James: "About the hourly rate... With our new guys... We start all laborers at $8.00 no matter what... Experience or not... We do this for 30 days. Then they get an evaluation and raise based on their performance. I've had too many people tell me they can do everything and they can do s***... But, I'll tell you straight up... Pull the trigger and hire someone... You're ready, and you need the experience of teaching someone how you want them to help run your business... It's not like you're in charge of someone else when you get a paycheck from a company... This is your money... Let me know how you make out..."

Join this discussion further here.

http://www.gophergraphics.com/forum/cgi-bin/ikonboard.cgi?act=ST;f=17;t=7966

GopherHaul business book – Stop Lowballing.

I just got our latest Gopher Lawn Care Business Book *"Stop Lowballing, A Lawn Care Business Owner's Guide To Success"* available online. It's 122 pages packed with great information we learned over the years on the forum.

You should get this book and read it to help yourself grow and succeed.

 To order the book visit our website http://www.gophergraphics.com or http://www.lawnchat.com or http://www.createspace.com/3342248 or check it out on amazon.com.

A discussion on quote cards and cross marketing.

Keith started off this great discussion by talking about how he uses his quote cards to market his lawn care business. Quote cards are cards you can create that include the services you offer, your contact information and they leave a spot for you to write in a quote to service that particular property. You can see the design Keith made in the link to this post's discussion.

Keith: "I made these cards and i go to a subdivision and put them in all the paper boxes with a quote for basic mowing.

They get printed on bright yellow paper on card stock I get 4 to a page (8 1/2 X 11) Costs are about $15.00 for 400 cards I have gotten about a 10% response! It's a lot of work but its paying off! I am out every free moment in the sub-divisions putting these in paper boxes."

Steve: "Do you put anything on the back of the card?"

Keith: "I am working on a co advertising program to charge a local pizza shop to put a coupon on the back and make a little money average yard is $25-$35."

Chuck: "I just did the same thing Friday.

I'm paying for the Pizzeria's menus to be reprinted & I get an ad on them. He sends them out with every delivery too. His current menus are 1 page black & white double sided print on basic white paper..... He folds them in half.... It couldn't get much cheaper! He asked if I would do his lawn for free pizza when I wanted it, I said I wouldn't use it often enough (it would take a lot of pizza) He

said then offer potential clients a free large pie once they sign up with you, you call me & I'll deliver it when ever they want.
Deal."

A note about this discussion. Chuck also was working at a quick lube center and he was able to set business cards on their counter. Chestin alludes to this in his next post.

Chestin of lawncaremarketingmagic: "I'd look to add some attention grabbing headline at the top of your card. Give them a reason to look at the card, then follow it up with some type of offer.

Don't just list your services. Give them a reason to actually pick up the phone and call.

It could be an introductory package at a discount. Or it could be a free oil change with a service contract. Or it could be....well, you get the idea. Be creative and give them a reason to actually pick up the phone and call you today."

If we have learned one thing here, it is to be resourceful. If you are working part-time somewhere, ask yourself, how can you take advantage of that business to promote your new business? As we see, Chuck was able to do that by promoting his lawn care business at the quick lube facility he worked at. We also learned the power of cross marketing with other local businesses as well to help lower your marketing costs.

If you'd like to join this discussion further and see the graphic designs the forum members posted, visit the post here.

http://www.gophergraphics.com/forum/cgi-bin/ikonboard.cgi?act=ST;f=8;t=7965

A lawn care business referral marketing tip.

Eric shared a great referral marketing idea that he used when he ran his lawn care business.

In the discussion Eric talked about how he would send out letters to his customers to help him gain more referrals clients.

Eric: "Back when a dollar meant something, I'd enclose a dollar bill and a business card. I'd ask them to refer a neighbor or friend nearby. The mowing service grew so big I had to sell it off after five years. I do miss those customers, and especially those monthly checks in the mail."

To take part in this discussion further, visit the post here.

http://www.gophergraphics.com/forum/cgi-bin/ikonboard.cgi? act=ST;f=9;t=7864

The Adventurers.

The adventurers.

This book would not have been complete without sharing the spotlight with my fellow adventurers in business and in life. Get on the Gopher Forum and say hi to them all. Each one my fellow adventurers is a shining example of what you can do when you put your mind to it. You can live the life you want. Dream it, Build it, Gopher it!

Justin Pitre - Just in Time Yard Services is operated and owned by Justin Pitre, a savvy 22 year old business man learning the tricks of the trade in the lawn care  industry. This business all started all back when I started to mow some lawns for a lawn care business/property management and they asked me if I wanted to mow the lawn that was on the property next door since the property to sale and there I was cutting grass for that property. Past experience was mostly grass cutting as I experienced that job for many years until I decided I had enough of minimum wage and start my own business. I thought at 20 years old, having a business would be tough to handle but I think I handled it pretty good since I had all that background experience. After receiving a $3,000 grant from the Canadian government, I told myself, if I can do this, I can run any business. My dad always told me, "You can do anything you want, as long you put your mind to it". Just in Time Yard Services is located in French River, ON, approximately 3.5 hrs north of Toronto, ON, Canada. I hope I've inspired some other teenagers to start there business, and this concludes my Just in Time Yard Services biography

You can visit our website at www.jitys.ca for more information

---

Keith Harper - Is owner and operator of the website:
www.StartALawnCareBusiness.com
Keith began his own lawn care business shortly after graduating college. He was working in the accounting department of a manufacturing company. Day after day, he longed to be outside instead of working in an office cubicle with no

windows.

With startup capital of only $150, Keith began his business in March 1992. By June, his business was in full swing and he was able to purchase his first commercial walk behind lawn mower.

Commercial lawn equipment gave Keith the ability to bid larger jobs and by 1995 he was successfully bidding and winning multi-year government mowing contracts. While actively pursuing large scale mowing contracts, he did not turn his back on his residential clientele and maintained a full roster of customers.

During the mid 2000's Keith began scaling back the cutting side of his lawn care business keeping only a select few residential customers.

Keith now spends much of his time developing software and authoring books for the lawn care industry. He is a strong advocate of young entrepreneurs and is devoted to helping them realize dreams of owning their own businesses.

In his free time, Keith is a kite enthusiast. He enjoys traveling to places such as the Grand Canyon where he practices the art of kite aerial photography.

Visit his website for more information on his lawn care business program, business software, lawn care estimating calculators, and training videos.

Website: www.StartALawnCareBusiness.com
Personal email: LawnCareBusiness@gmail.com

Ben Belhorn - Founded Gotta Mow Lawn Maintenance in the summer of 2008, with a belief that he had the energy, drive, determination and skills to get a small lawn care company off the ground.... Or perhaps on the ground would be a better term. Ben had been looking for a second job to supplement his income from his full time job and had been running into some difficulties. You see Ben works third shift for the Ohio Department of Transportation (ODOT) and whatever job he takes would have to go away in the winter. During the winter months ODOT employees frequently work 16 hour shifts plowing snow and spreading salt on the highways. But during the summer months the Outpost that Ben works at goes to 4, 10 hour shifts. So what could he do that would allow him the freedom to stop working every winter, work shorter hours part of the week during the summer, and work some weekends?

Ben decided to look to his background to see if there is anything there:

    - Over 8 years working in every possible position in the grocery business from bagger to manager.
    Wal-Mart is always hiring, No thanks

    - 3 years as a Sheriffs deputy
    He could become a part time freelance police officer. That's called a vigilante. Bad idea.

    - 5 years owning a One hour photolab and digital imaging center.
    He stopped doing that because he was not making any money. Now do it for minimum wage?

Think think thin.... Wait he got it!! A job that allows him to work at his own schedule goes away in the winter and is inexpensive to start. Lawn Care!

So Gotta Mow is started with what he had a brand new Craftsman 22" mower and a Craftsman trimmer. Along with some stuff out of his garage all loaded into the back of his 99 Chevy Tahoe.

Advertising on Craigslist with good, professional looking ads, put together a website, and made some business cards. Then his cell phone started ringing and emails started coming.

Less than a month into this little venture and he had already developed 3 weekly customers who signed contracts for the year. He had been called for estimates for several properties that were too large for him to handle, and was being forced to look into expanding his equipment.

He realized... He could expand his client list much faster than he could procure equipment. This is going to be fun and challenging.

For more on the Saga visit www.GottaMowOhio.com or just call Ben on his cell phone and ask how he's doing 614-271-0188

Chuck Cantasano - Is a 30 yr old Floridian transplant (moved from Long Island N.Y. about 19 years ago).
By day he is an business owner running a lawn care / landscaping company in Charlotte County Florida. He is married & a father of two young children one girl, one boy. On top of that he has yet to let go of music which has been his passion since childhood. He is the lead guitarist & vocalist for an all original rock band called Jack
Somebody. Running a family, then a business, then a band (in that order of importance) gets tiresome at times but I love all three.

The business is getting better all the time, which makes family life nicer and I have more time to enjoy my wife and kids now, The band has gained more notoriety playing shows from Tampa down through Ft. Myers & the release of our 2nd cd seems to have some fan anticipation at least regionally so all is good!

Blaine & Shelley Dennison - Quick & Clean Lawn Care LLC

In the mist of hurricane Katina Quick & Clean lawn care was founded by owners, Blaine and Shelley Dennison. Armed with only a hand-me-down mower and a broom, we started advertising on local yahoo groups, like craiglist, and Lakeview rebuild.

By the summer of '06 we had over 20 customers across The New Orleans metro area. Over the summer we upgraded our equipment to a John Deere EZ Trac ZTR Echo brand trimmer and hand held blower.

Today Quick & Clean Lawn Care is now an LLC and is progressively growing and upgrading. Now equipped with 2 John Deeres, echo weed trimmers and back pack blowers we continue to service the still storm ravaged New Orleans area with quality work.

Anyone needing our services in Orleans or Jefferson Parsh, can fill free to call Blaine or Shelley @ (504) 469-7121
Or email Quickcleanlawn@bellsouth.net

Tara Gray – Green Paws Lawn Care - http://www.greenpawslawncare.com

Chestin Salisbury – Lawn Care Marketing Magic
http://lawncaremarketingmagic.com/

Ken LaVoie – Lawn Care Business Author http://www.lawnguru.net/

Brandon Little is the Owner of Little's Tree Works and http://www.littlestreeworks.com. He started a lawn care business in 2003 after ending a career in retail management.

With the business management experience and a longing to work outdoors, he took his savings and invested it in the necessary equipment needed to start and operate a lawn care business based on excellent customer service principles, and takes pride in his work.

After majoring in Horticulture he found his love for working with trees. He began studying and practicing proper tree services and now works solely in and

around trees, and enjoys tree climbing as a hobby, along with photography, mt. biking, and fishing around his hometown of Redding, CA. with his beautiful wife Christina, and his 3 lovely kids.
Brandon can be reached through his website at http://www.littlestreeworks.com